Welcome guests

May all who enter as guests, leave as friends!

Montagne

Rochers

Chemin Vicinal

Pont sur le Ch.in de Fer

Talus en déblais

Tunnel

Monticule

Signal

Île

Source

Carrières

Hameau

Landes

Ruisseau

Bruyères

Usine

Confluent

Digue

Fonderie

Bac à traille

Bac

Fossés d'irrigation

Pont tout en bois (cours d'eau)

Maison

Gué à pied

Pont en bois avec piles

Prairies

Gué à chevaux

Rivière

Bo

VILLE

Chemin

Ferme

Vanne

Pont en pierre

Embranchement

Sentier

Gare

Étang

Vignes

Vignes

Avant Pont

Pont sous le Ch.in de Fer

Talus en remblai

Route

Départementale

Jardins et Vergers

de

Route Nationale

Village

Sables et Dunes

La

Fleuve

Phare

Embouchure

Fer

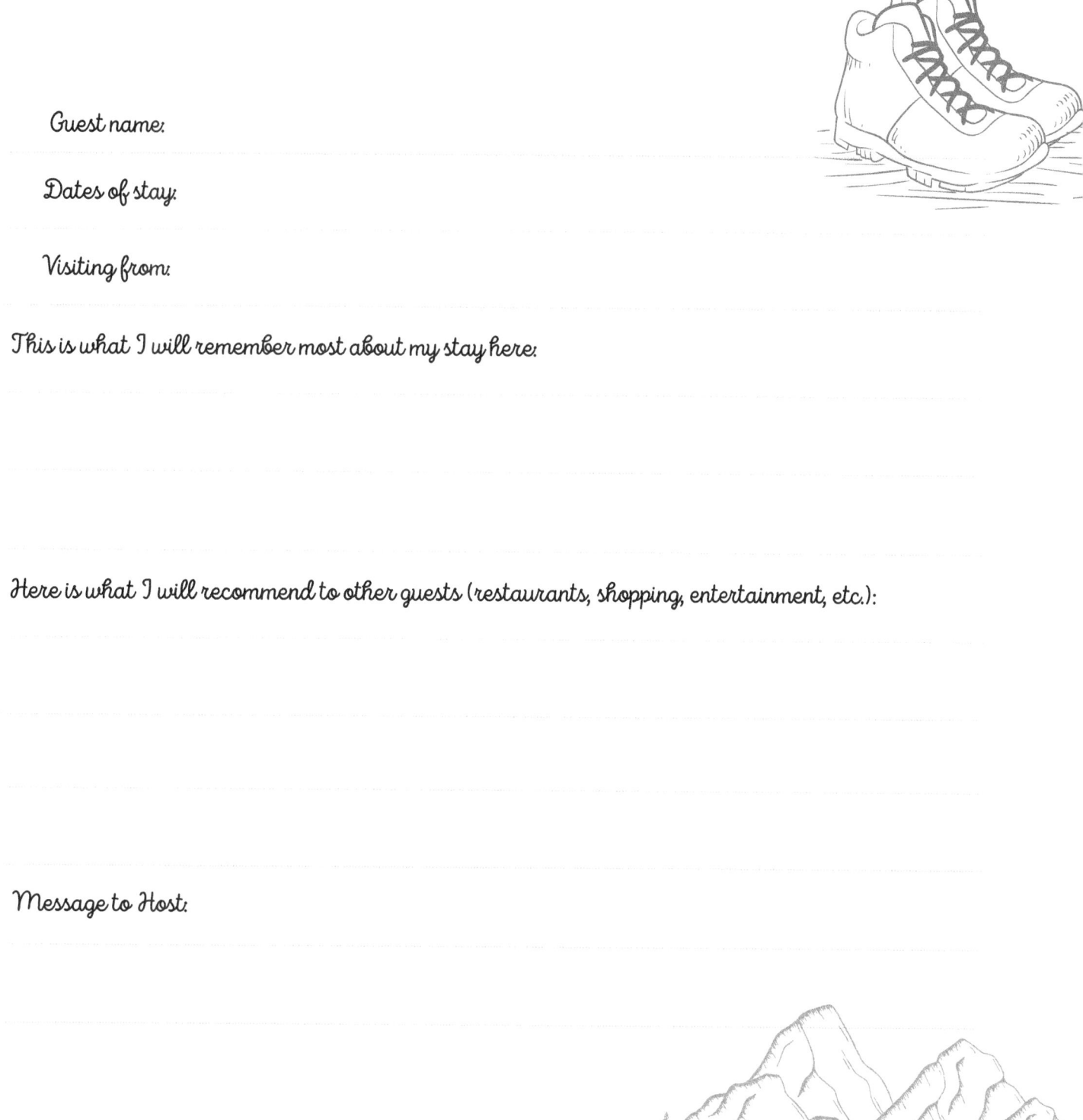

Guest name:

Dates of stay:

Visiting from:

This is what I will remember most about my stay here:

Here is what I will recommend to other guests (restaurants, shopping, entertainment, etc.):

Message to Host:

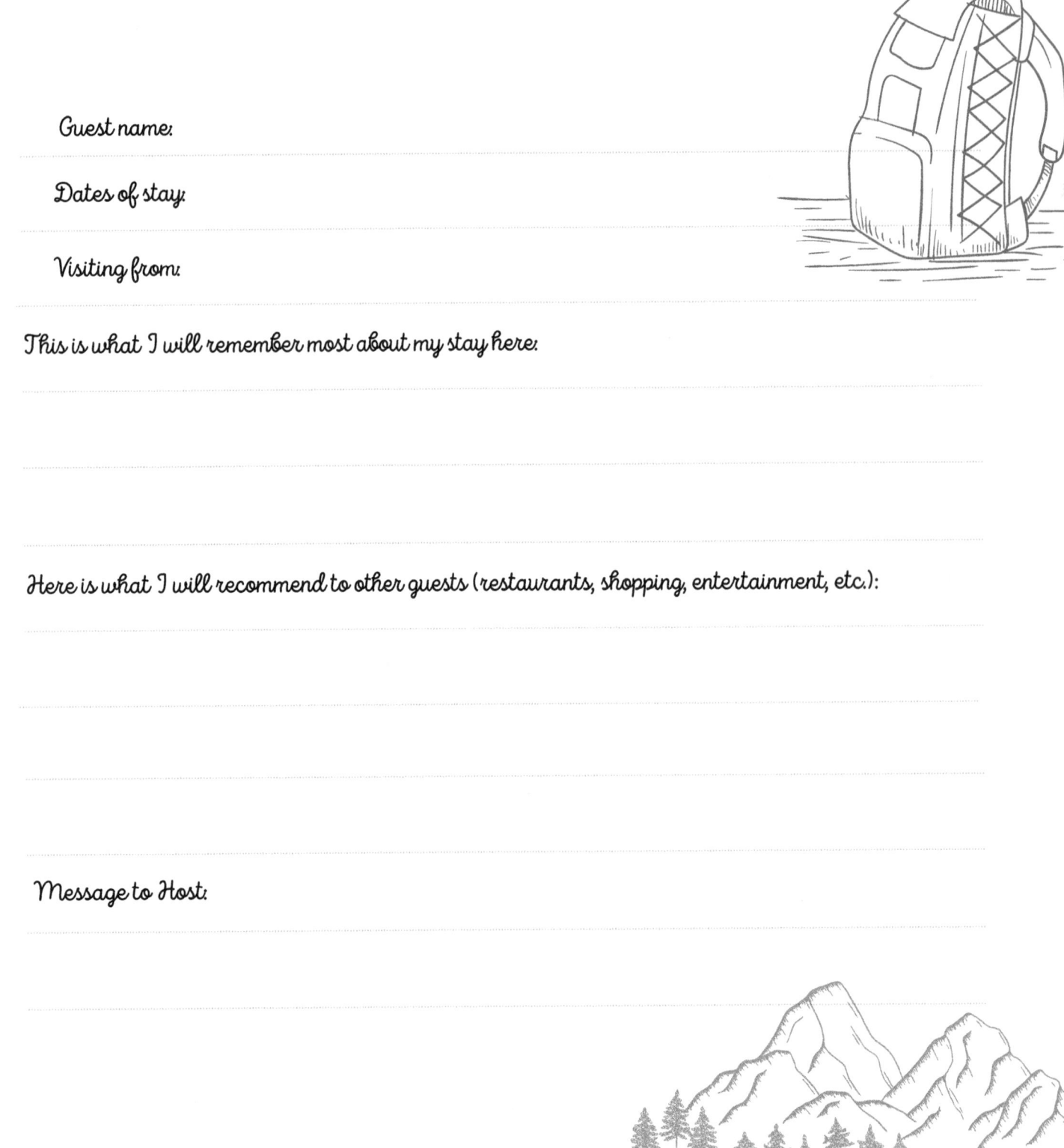

Guest name:

Dates of stay:

Visiting from:

This is what I will remember most about my stay here:

Here is what I will recommend to other guests (restaurants, shopping, entertainment, etc.):

Message to Host:

Guest name:

Dates of stay:

Visiting from:

This is what I will remember most about my stay here:

Here is what I will recommend to other guests (restaurants, shopping, entertainment, etc.):

Message to Host:

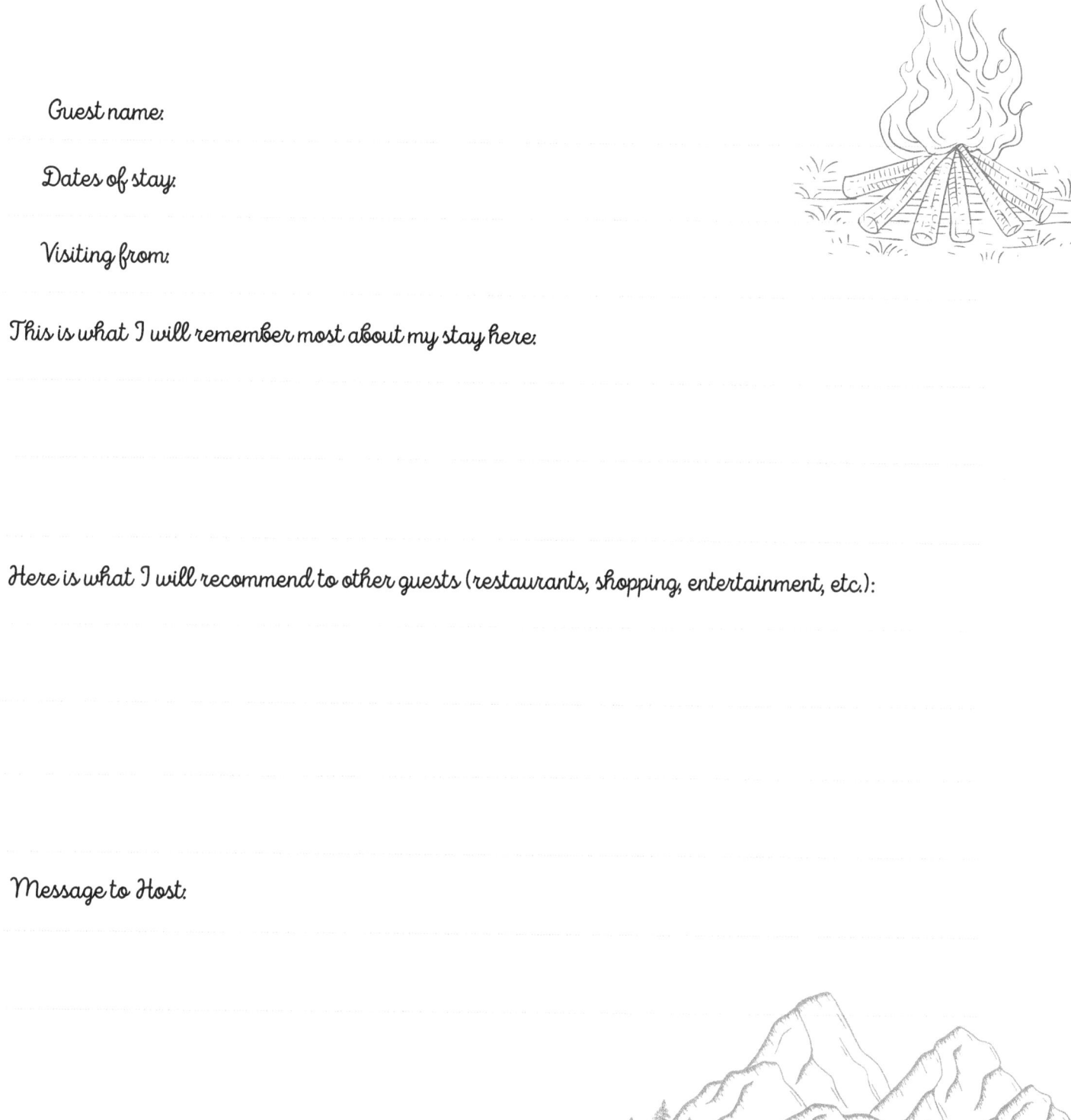

Guest name:

Dates of stay:

Visiting from:

This is what I will remember most about my stay here:

Here is what I will recommend to other guests (restaurants, shopping, entertainment, etc.):

Message to Host:

Guest name:

Dates of stay:

Visiting from:

This is what I will remember most about my stay here:

Here is what I will recommend to other guests (restaurants, shopping, entertainment, etc.):

Message to Host:

Guest name:

Dates of stay:

Visiting from:

This is what I will remember most about my stay here:

Here is what I will recommend to other guests (restaurants, shopping, entertainment, etc.):

Message to Host:

Guest name:

Dates of stay:

Visiting from:

This is what I will remember most about my stay here:

Here is what I will recommend to other guests (restaurants, shopping, entertainment, etc.):

Message to Host:

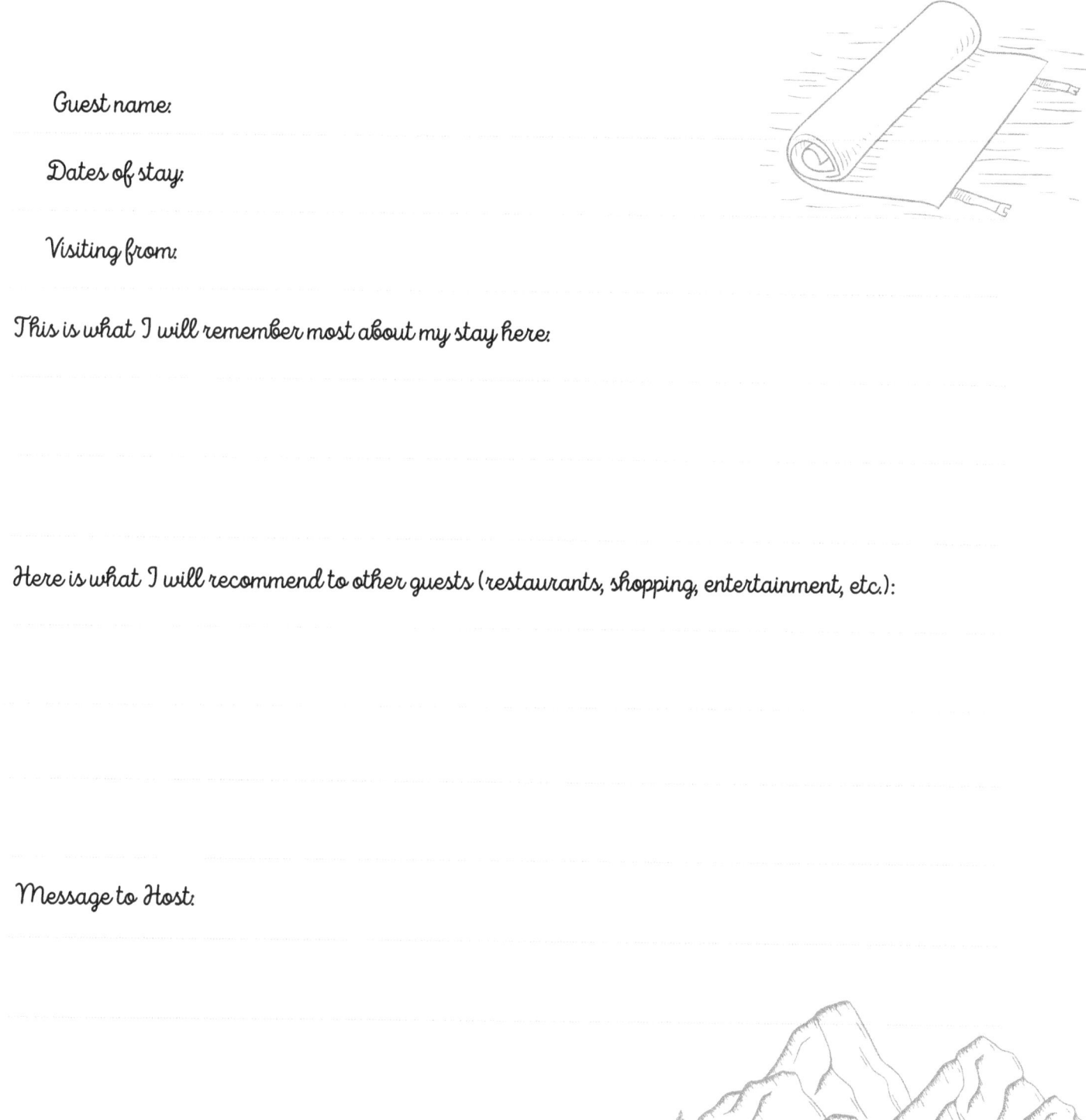

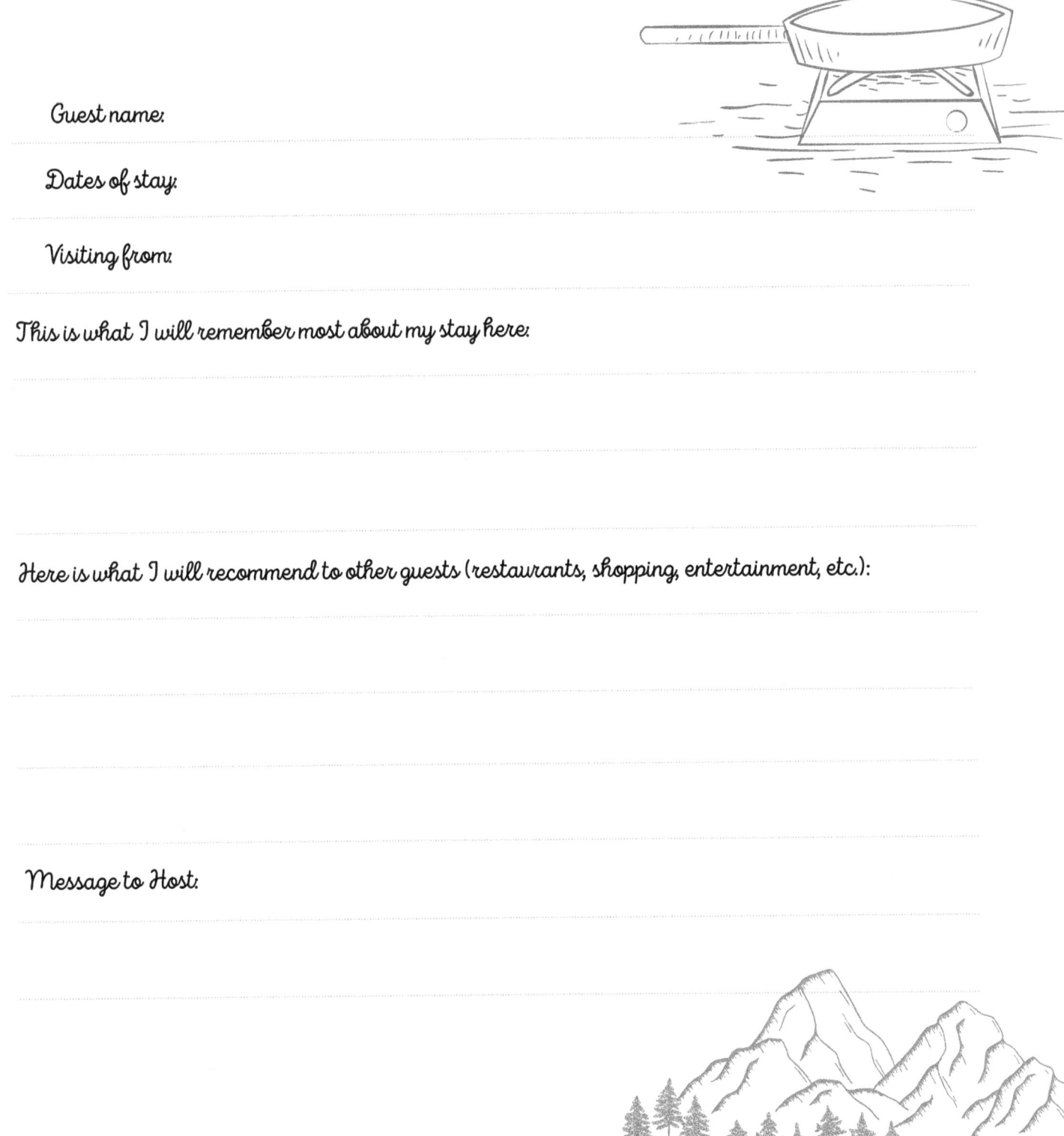

Guest name:

Dates of stay:

Visiting from:

This is what I will remember most about my stay here:

Here is what I will recommend to other guests (restaurants, shopping, entertainment, etc.):

Message to Host:

Guest name:

Dates of stay:

Visiting from:

This is what I will remember most about my stay here:

Here is what I will recommend to other guests (restaurants, shopping, entertainment, etc.):

Message to Host:

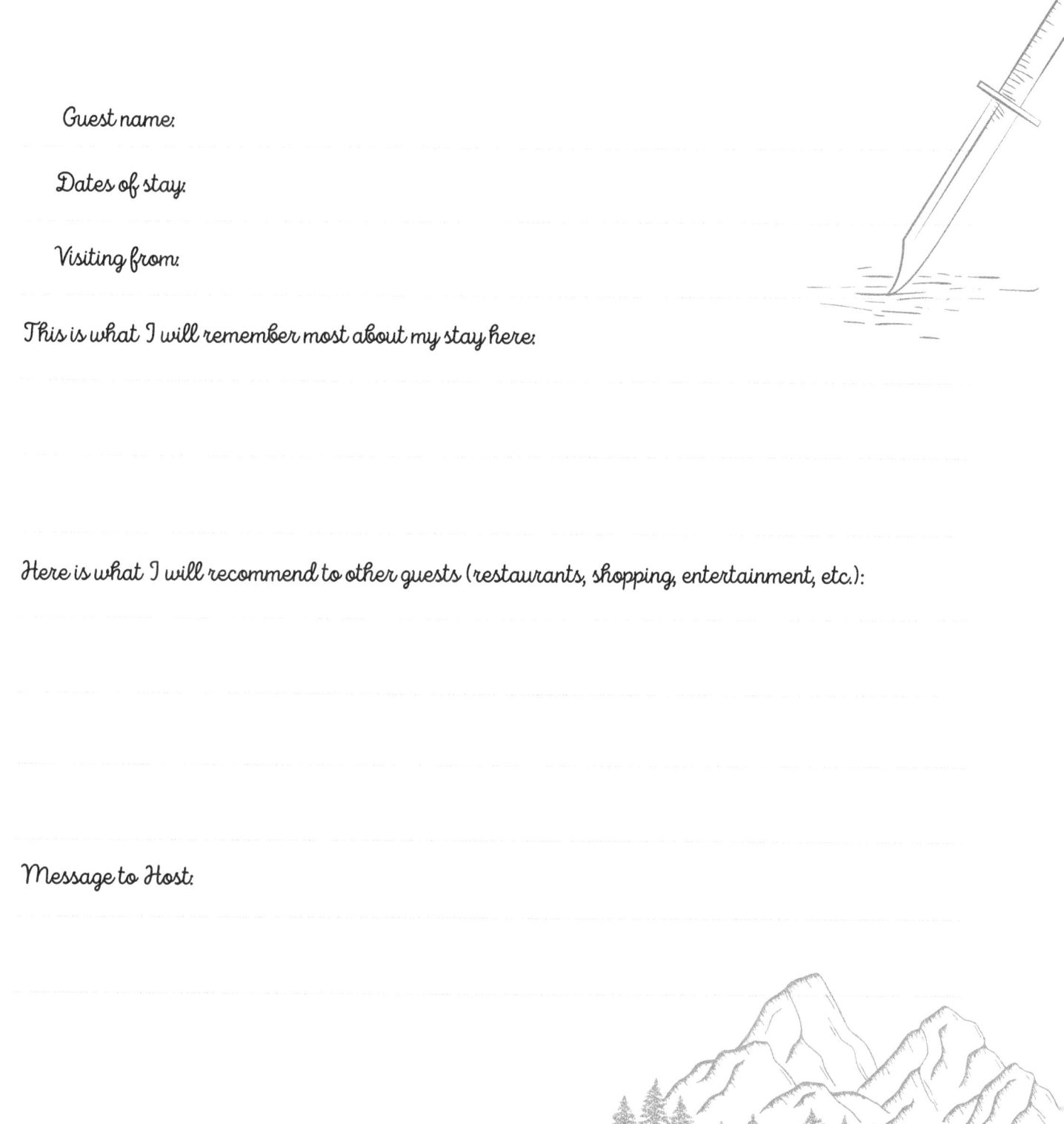

Guest name:

Dates of stay:

Visiting from:

This is what I will remember most about my stay here:

Here is what I will recommend to other guests (restaurants, shopping, entertainment, etc.):

Message to Host:

Guest name:

Dates of stay:

Visiting from:

This is what I will remember most about my stay here:

Here is what I will recommend to other guests (restaurants, shopping, entertainment, etc.):

Message to Host:

Guest name:

Dates of stay:

Visiting from:

This is what I will remember most about my stay here:

Here is what I will recommend to other guests (restaurants, shopping, entertainment, etc.):

Message to Host:

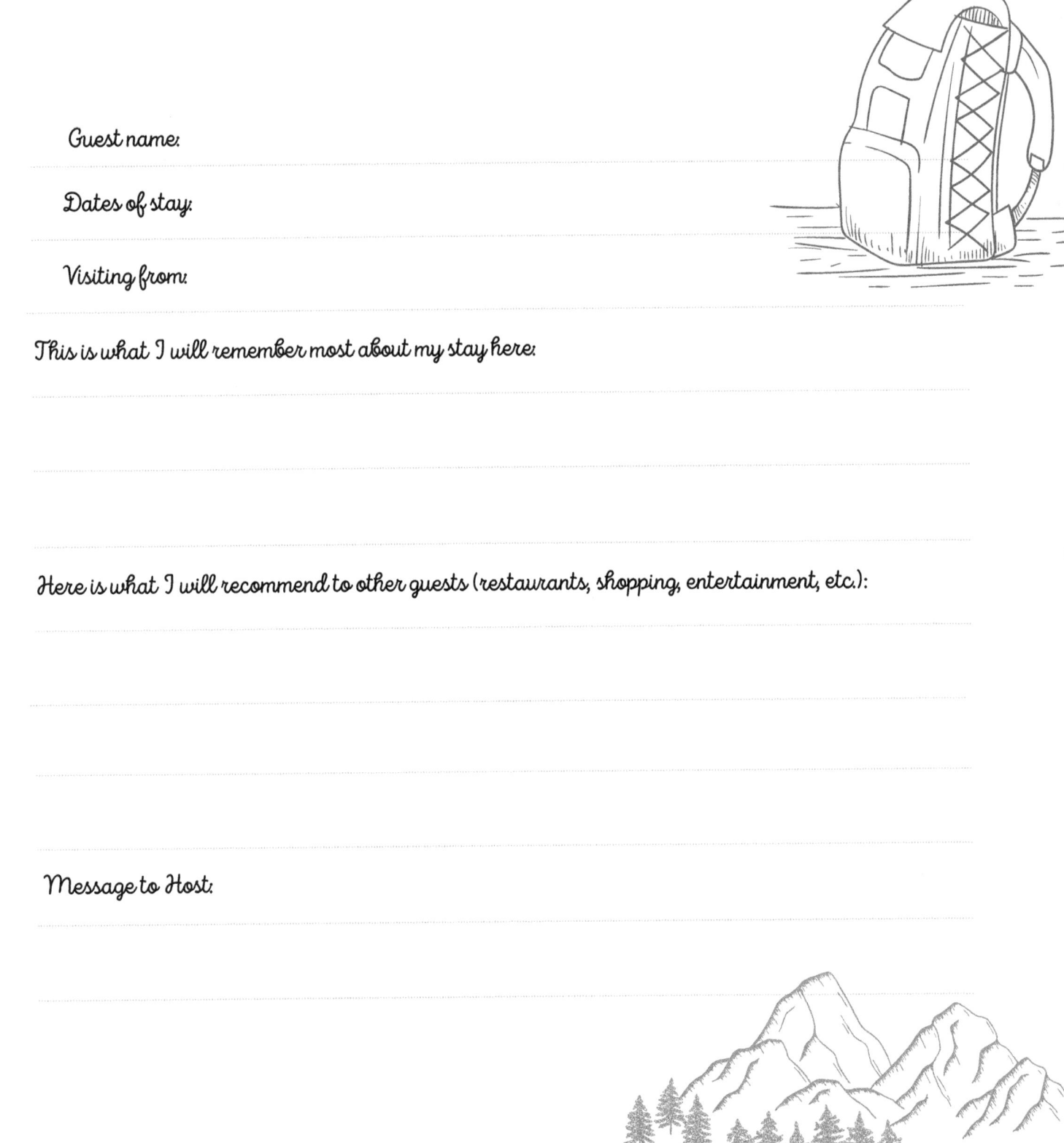

Guest name:

Dates of stay:

Visiting from:

This is what I will remember most about my stay here:

Here is what I will recommend to other guests (restaurants, shopping, entertainment, etc.):

Message to Host:

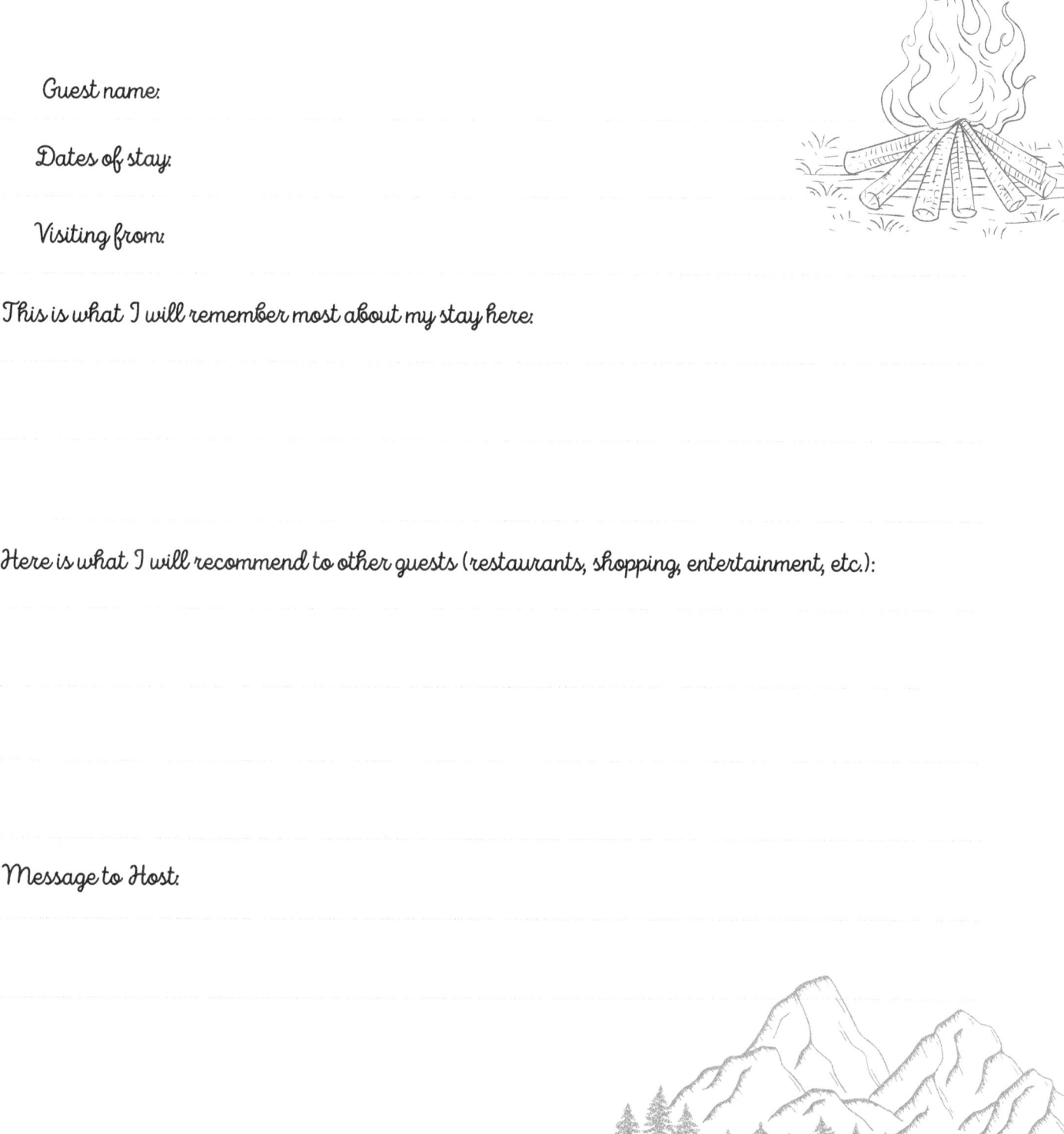

Guest name:

Dates of stay:

Visiting from:

This is what I will remember most about my stay here:

Here is what I will recommend to other guests (restaurants, shopping, entertainment, etc.):

Message to Host:

Guest name:

Dates of stay:

Visiting from:

This is what I will remember most about my stay here:

Here is what I will recommend to other guests (restaurants, shopping, entertainment, etc.):

Message to Host:

Guest name:

Dates of stay:

Visiting from:

This is what I will remember most about my stay here:

Here is what I will recommend to other guests (restaurants, shopping, entertainment, etc.):

Message to Host:

Guest name:

Dates of stay:

Visiting from:

This is what I will remember most about my stay here:

Here is what I will recommend to other guests (restaurants, shopping, entertainment, etc.):

Message to Host:

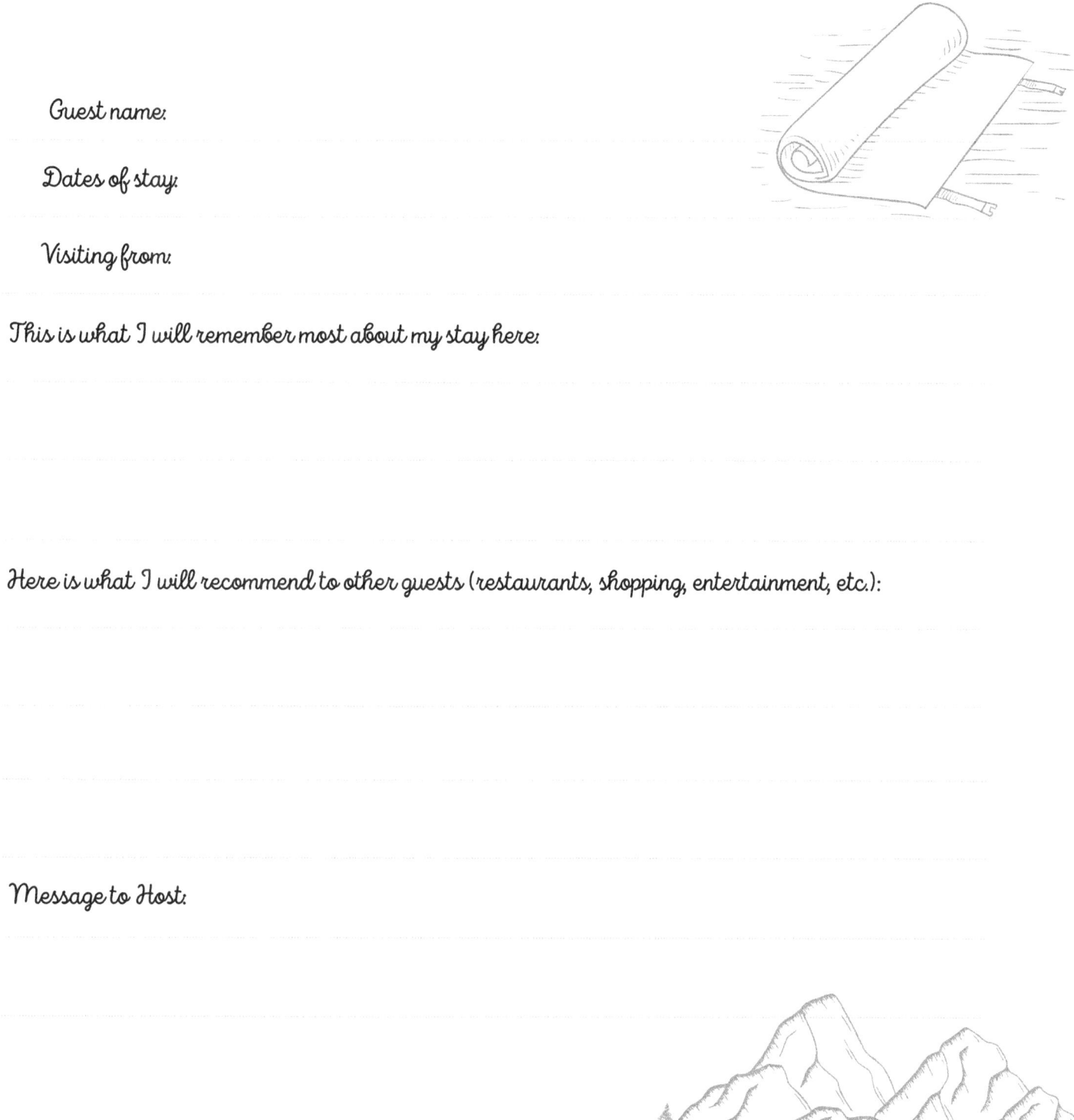

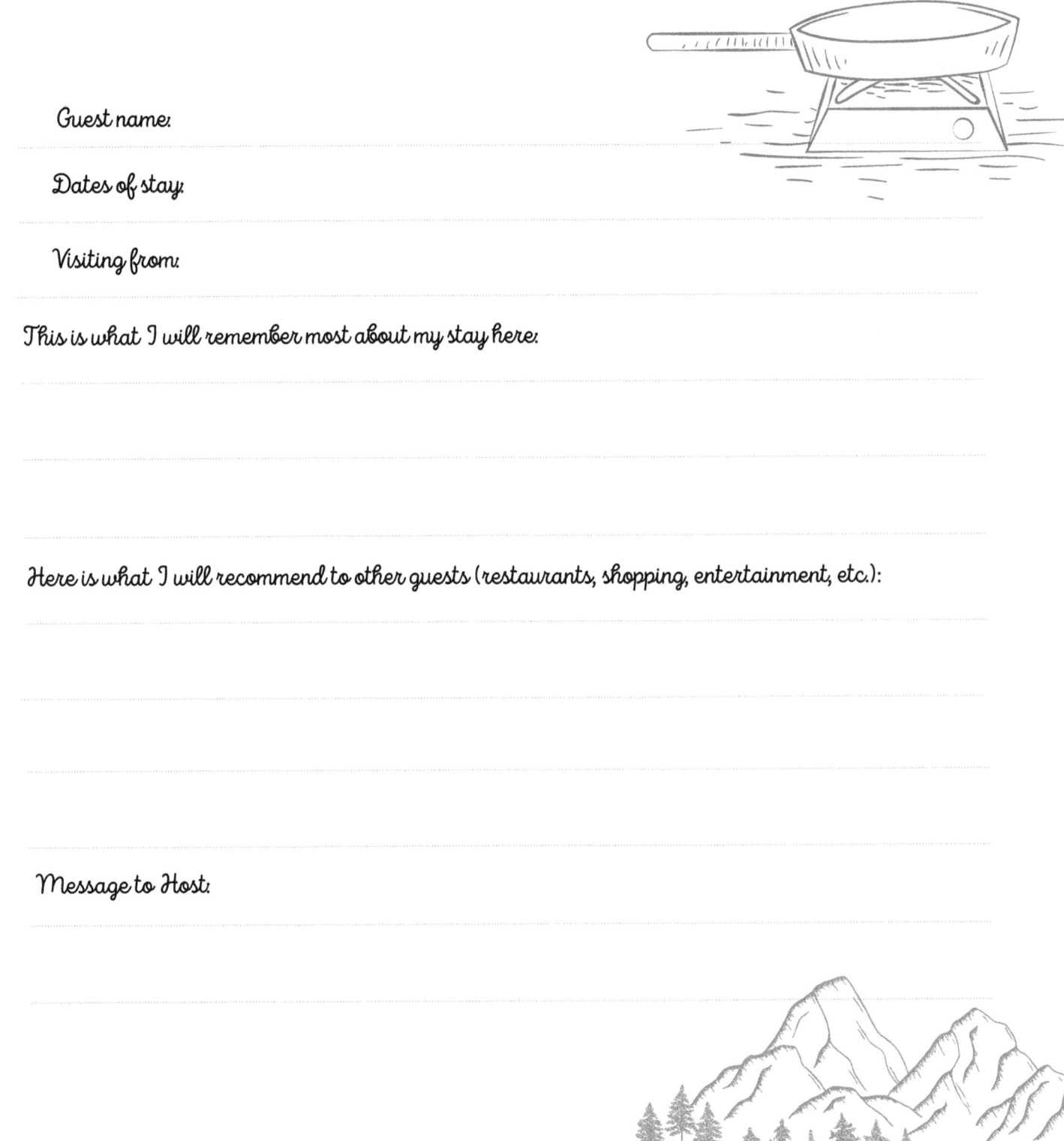

Guest name:

Dates of stay:

Visiting from:

This is what I will remember most about my stay here:

Here is what I will recommend to other guests (restaurants, shopping, entertainment, etc.):

Message to Host:

Guest name:

Dates of stay:

Visiting from:

This is what I will remember most about my stay here:

Here is what I will recommend to other guests (restaurants, shopping, entertainment, etc.):

Message to Host:

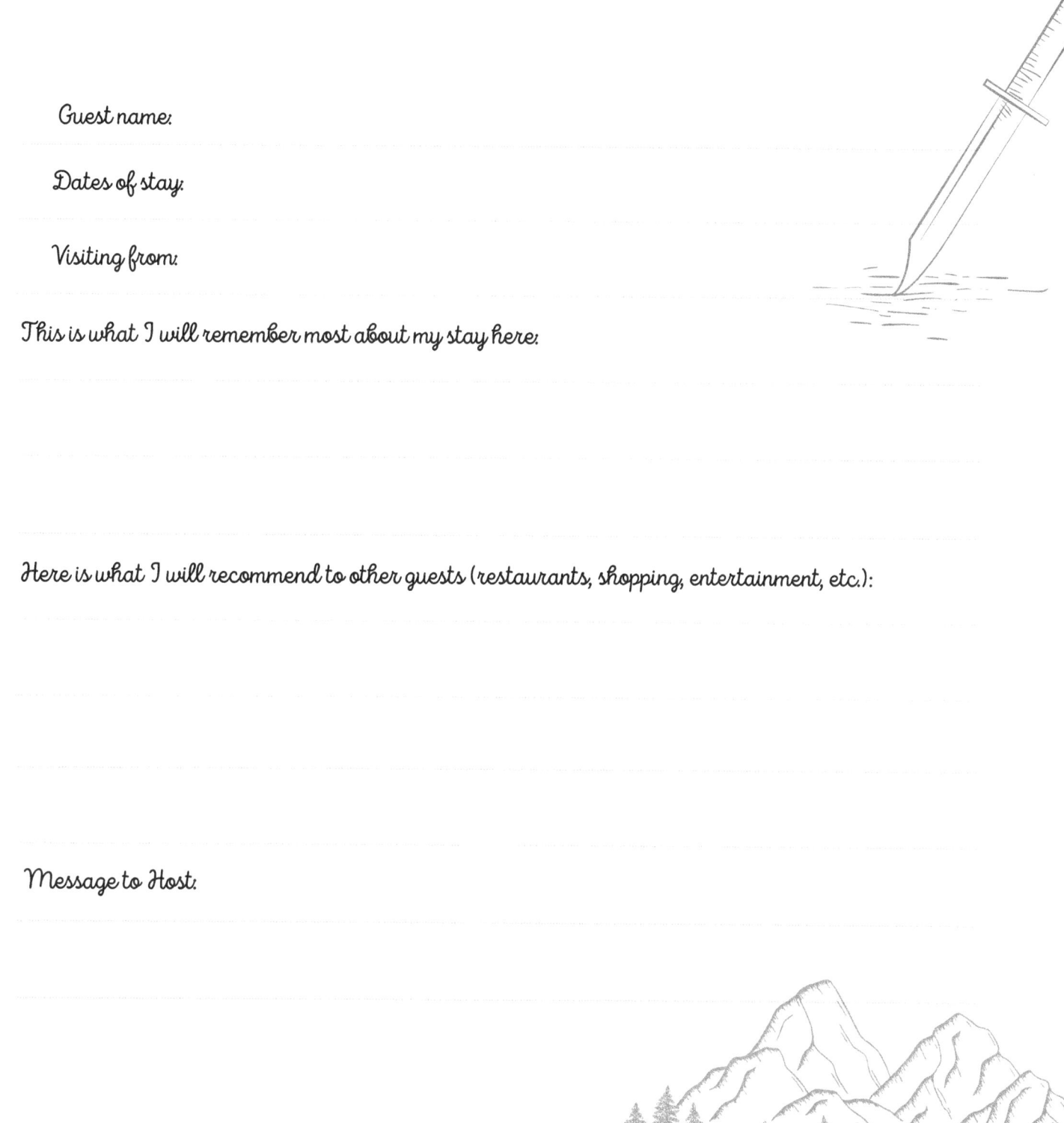

Guest name:

Dates of stay:

Visiting from:

This is what I will remember most about my stay here:

Here is what I will recommend to other guests (restaurants, shopping, entertainment, etc.):

Message to Host:

Guest name:

Dates of stay:

Visiting from:

This is what I will remember most about my stay here:

Here is what I will recommend to other guests (restaurants, shopping, entertainment, etc.):

Message to Host:

Guest name:

Dates of stay:

Visiting from:

This is what I will remember most about my stay here:

Here is what I will recommend to other guests (restaurants, shopping, entertainment, etc.):

Message to Host:

Guest name:

Dates of stay:

Visiting from:

This is what I will remember most about my stay here:

Here is what I will recommend to other guests (restaurants, shopping, entertainment, etc.):

Message to Host:

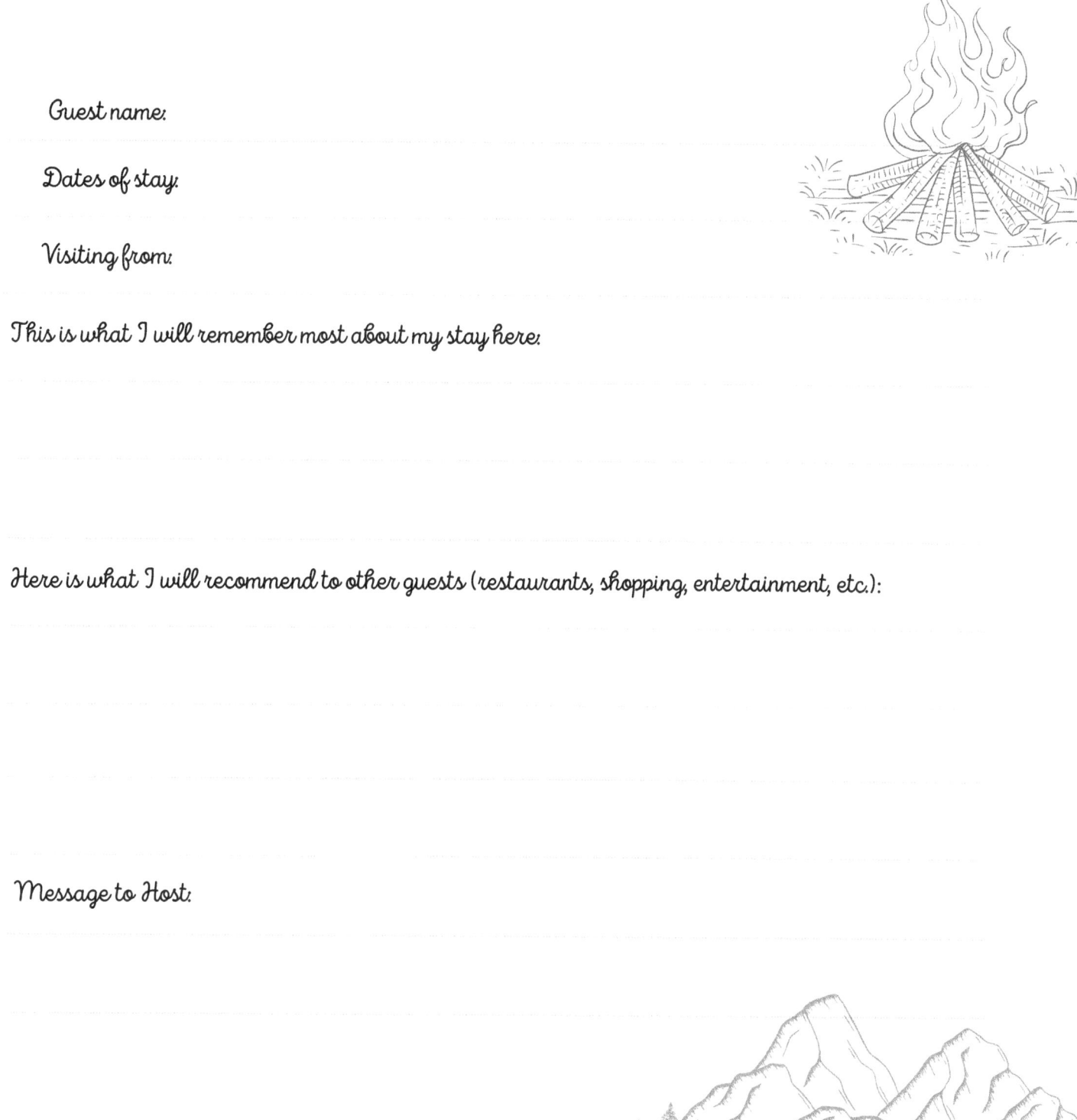

Guest name:

Dates of stay:

Visiting from:

This is what I will remember most about my stay here:

Here is what I will recommend to other guests (restaurants, shopping, entertainment, etc.):

Message to Host:

Guest name:

Dates of stay:

Visiting from:

This is what I will remember most about my stay here:

Here is what I will recommend to other guests (restaurants, shopping, entertainment, etc.):

Message to Host:

Guest name:

Dates of stay:

Visiting from:

This is what I will remember most about my stay here:

Here is what I will recommend to other guests (restaurants, shopping, entertainment, etc.):

Message to Host:

Guest name:

Dates of stay:

Visiting from:

This is what I will remember most about my stay here:

Here is what I will recommend to other guests (restaurants, shopping, entertainment, etc.):

Message to Host:

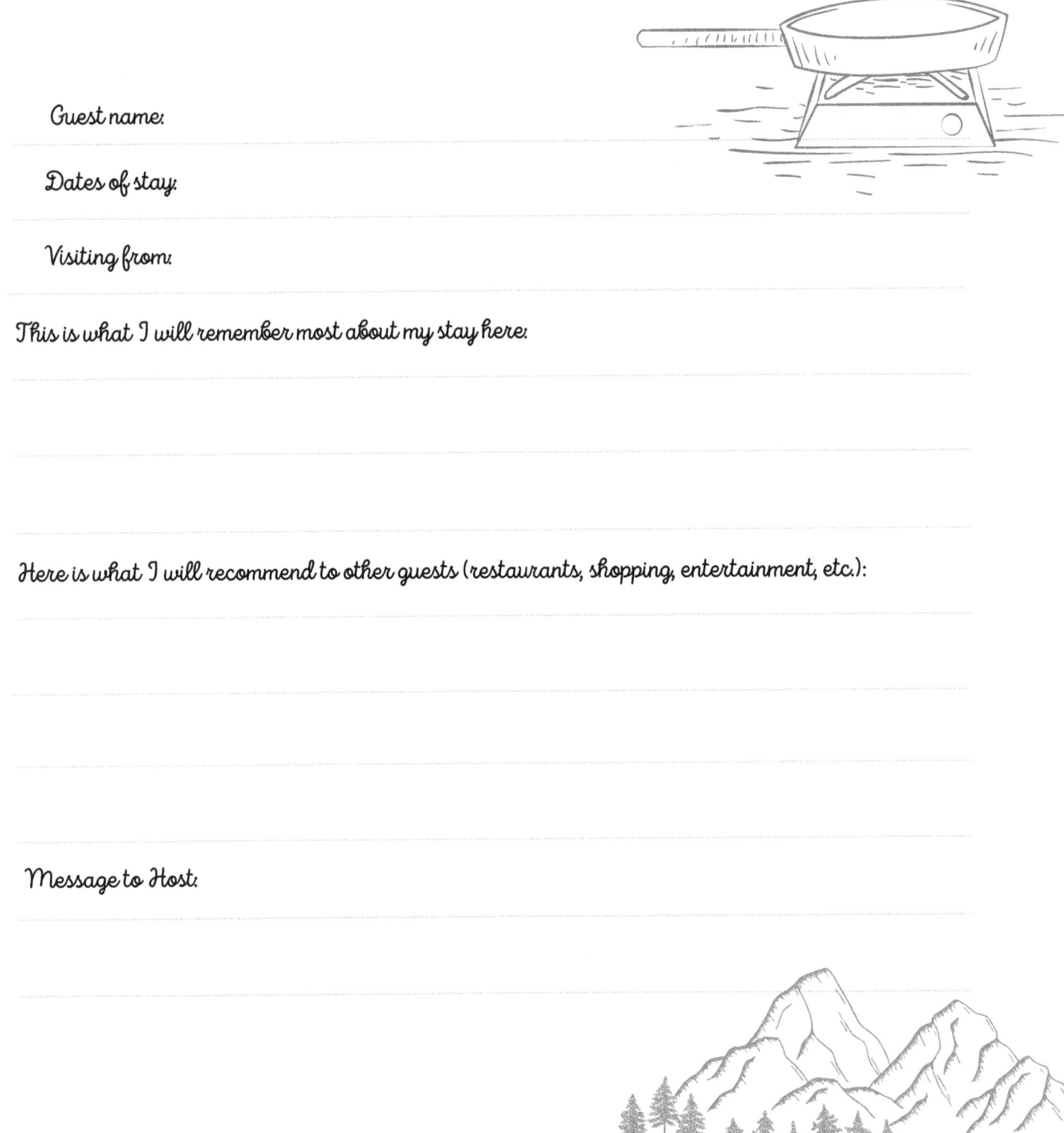

Guest name:

Dates of stay:

Visiting from:

This is what I will remember most about my stay here:

Here is what I will recommend to other guests (restaurants, shopping, entertainment, etc.):

Message to Host:

Guest name:

Dates of stay:

Visiting from:

This is what I will remember most about my stay here:

Here is what I will recommend to other guests (restaurants, shopping, entertainment, etc.):

Message to Host:

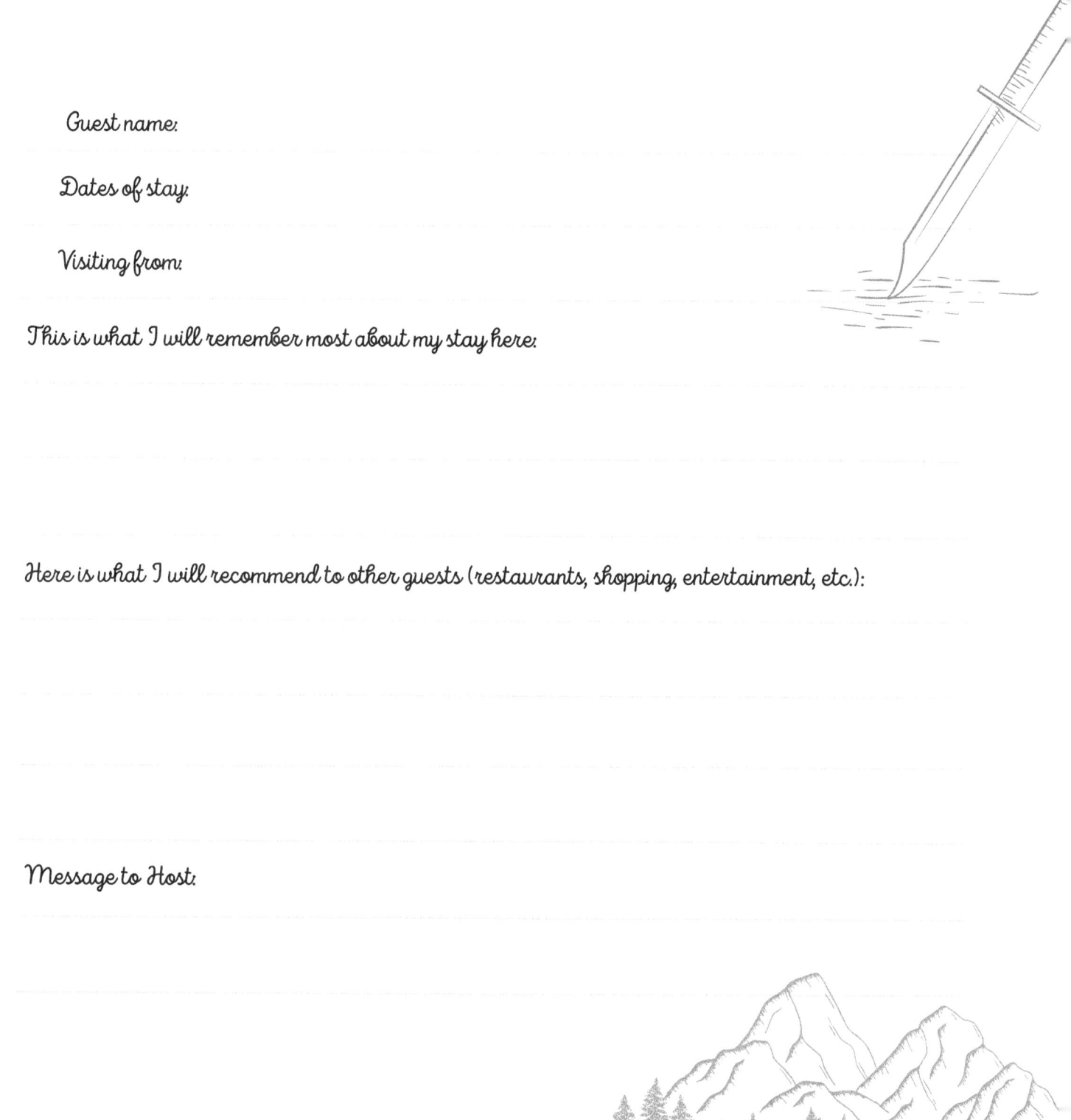

Guest name:

Dates of stay:

Visiting from:

This is what I will remember most about my stay here:

Here is what I will recommend to other guests (restaurants, shopping, entertainment, etc.):

Message to Host:

Guest name:

Dates of stay:

Visiting from:

This is what I will remember most about my stay here:

Here is what I will recommend to other guests (restaurants, shopping, entertainment, etc.):

Message to Host:

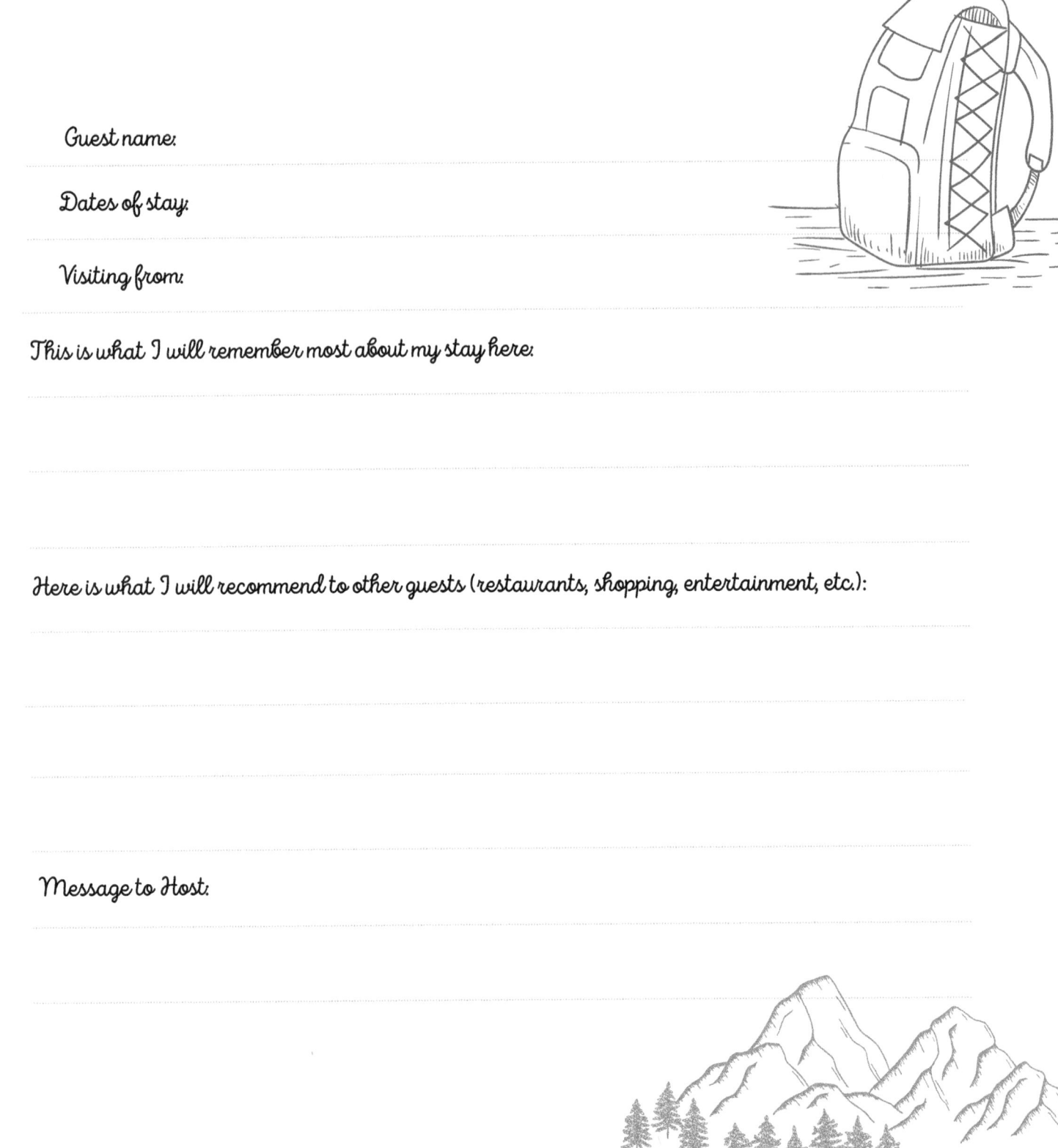

Guest name:

Dates of stay:

Visiting from:

This is what I will remember most about my stay here:

Here is what I will recommend to other guests (restaurants, shopping, entertainment, etc.):

Message to Host:

Guest name:

Dates of stay:

Visiting from:

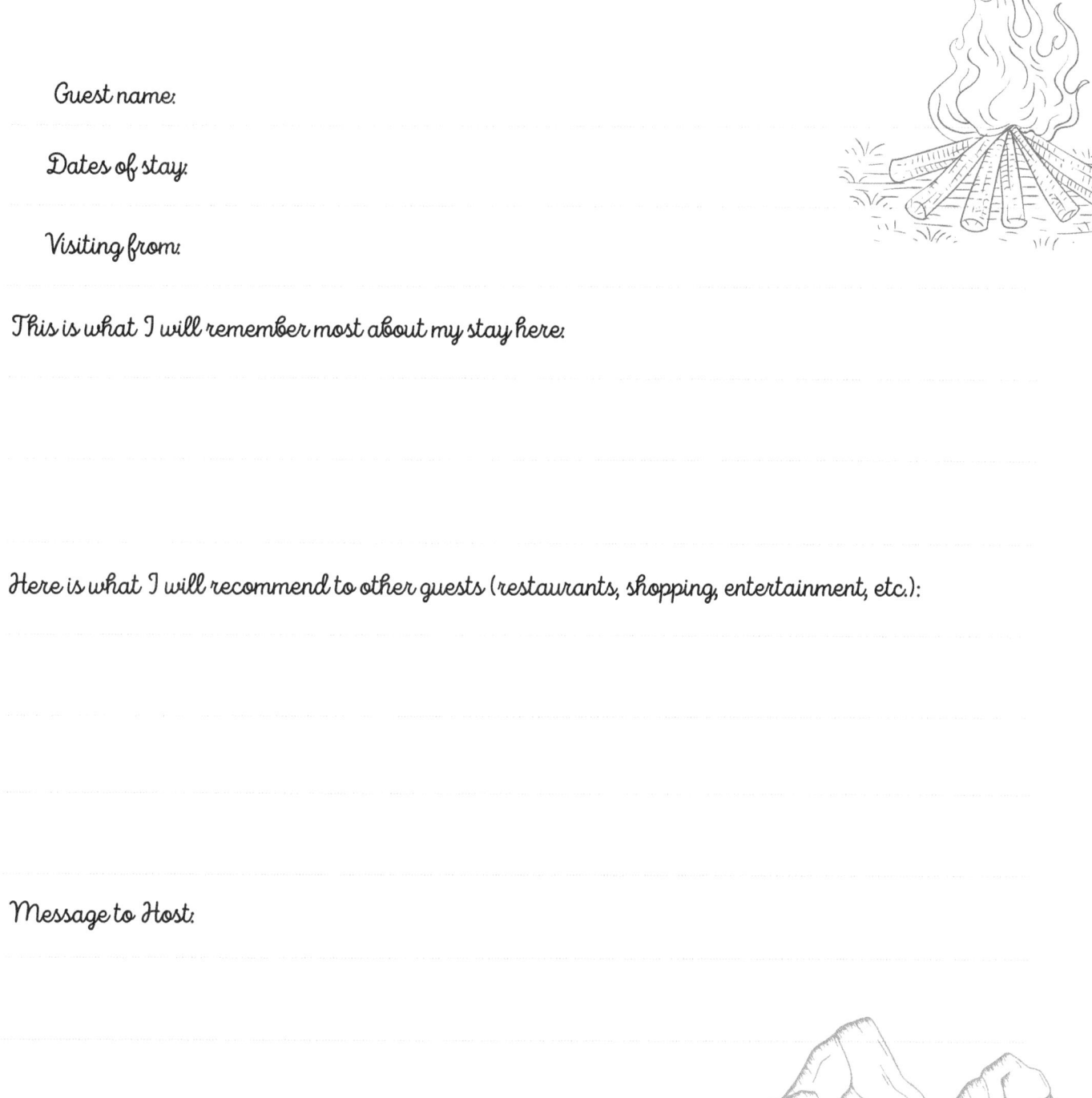

This is what I will remember most about my stay here:

Here is what I will recommend to other guests (restaurants, shopping, entertainment, etc.):

Message to Host:

Guest name:

Dates of stay:

Visiting from:

This is what I will remember most about my stay here:

Here is what I will recommend to other guests (restaurants, shopping, entertainment, etc.):

Message to Host:

Guest name:

Dates of stay:

Visiting from:

This is what I will remember most about my stay here:

Here is what I will recommend to other guests (restaurants, shopping, entertainment, etc.):

Message to Host:

Guest name:

Dates of stay:

Visiting from:

This is what I will remember most about my stay here:

Here is what I will recommend to other guests (restaurants, shopping, entertainment, etc.):

Message to Host:

Guest name:

Dates of stay:

Visiting from:

This is what I will remember most about my stay here:

Here is what I will recommend to other guests (restaurants, shopping, entertainment, etc.):

Message to Host:

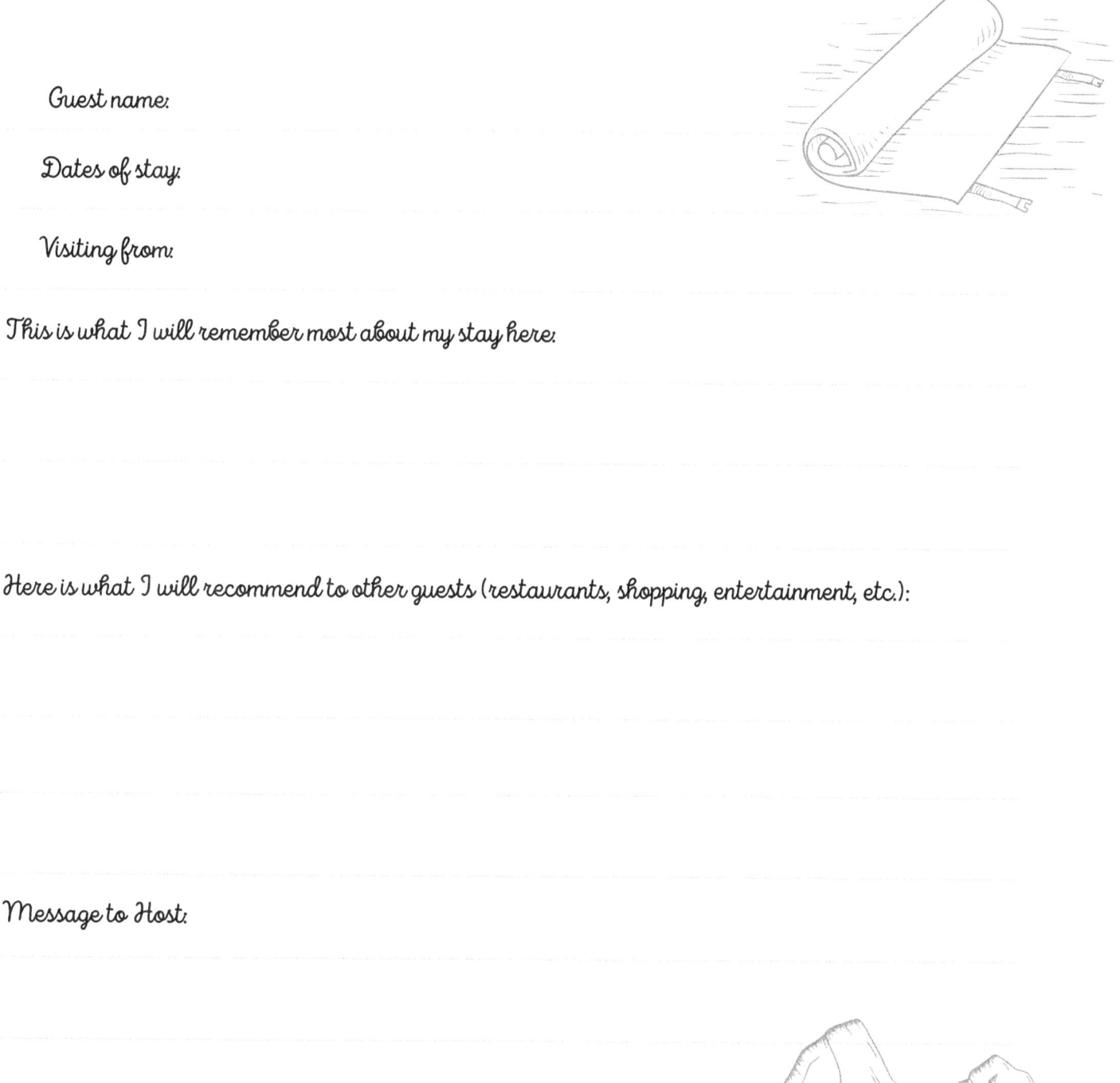

Guest name:

Dates of stay:

Visiting from:

This is what I will remember most about my stay here:

Here is what I will recommend to other guests (restaurants, shopping, entertainment, etc.):

Message to Host:

Guest name:

Dates of stay:

Visiting from:

This is what I will remember most about my stay here:

Here is what I will recommend to other guests (restaurants, shopping, entertainment, etc.):

Message to Host:

Guest name:

Dates of stay:

Visiting from:

This is what I will remember most about my stay here:

Here is what I will recommend to other guests (restaurants, shopping, entertainment, etc.):

Message to Host:

Guest name:

Dates of stay:

Visiting from:

This is what I will remember most about my stay here:

Here is what I will recommend to other guests (restaurants, shopping, entertainment, etc.):

Message to Host:

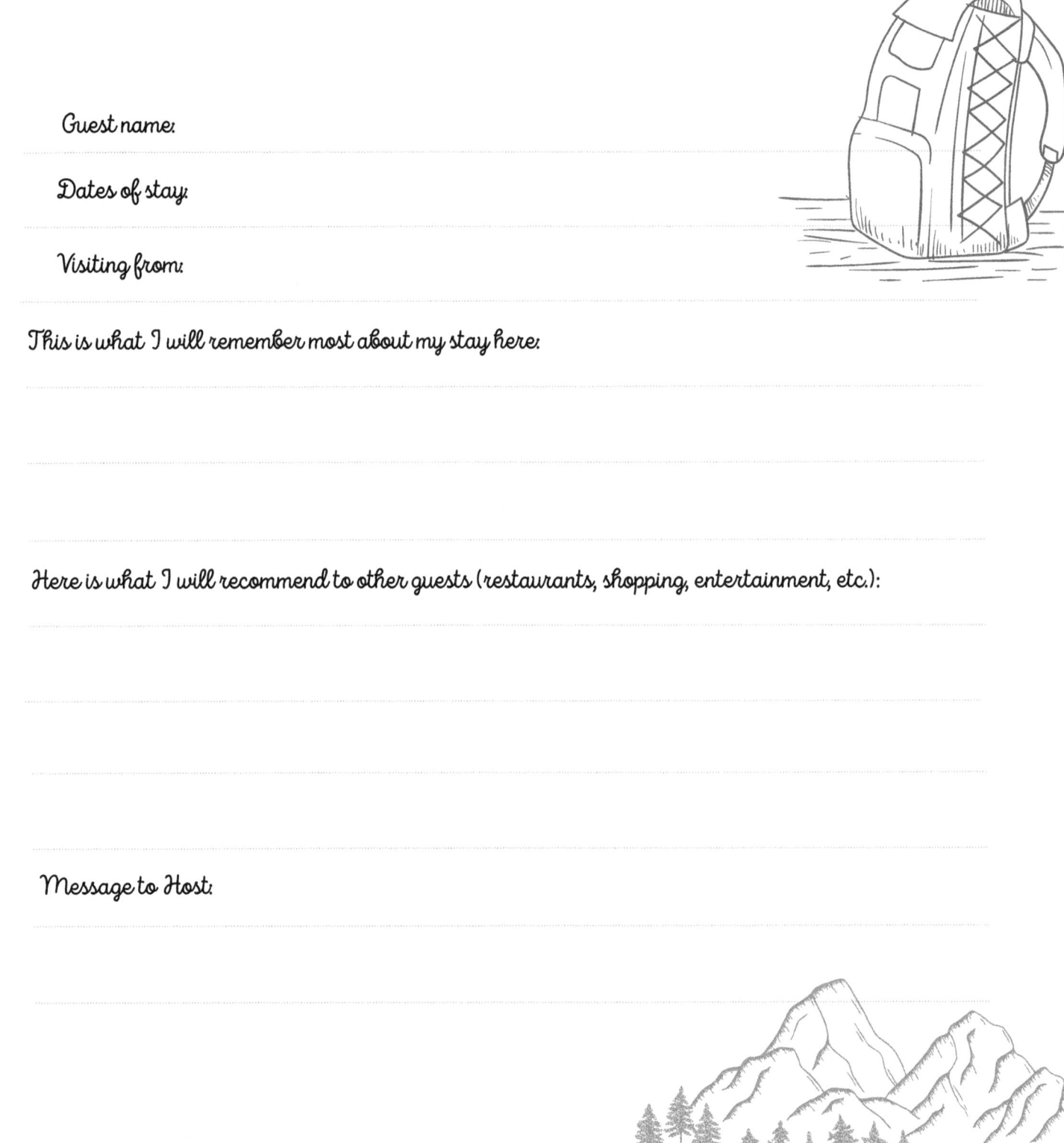

Guest name:

Dates of stay:

Visiting from:

This is what I will remember most about my stay here:

Here is what I will recommend to other guests (restaurants, shopping, entertainment, etc.):

Message to Host:

Guest name:

Dates of stay:

Visiting from:

This is what I will remember most about my stay here:

Here is what I will recommend to other guests (restaurants, shopping, entertainment, etc.):

Message to Host:

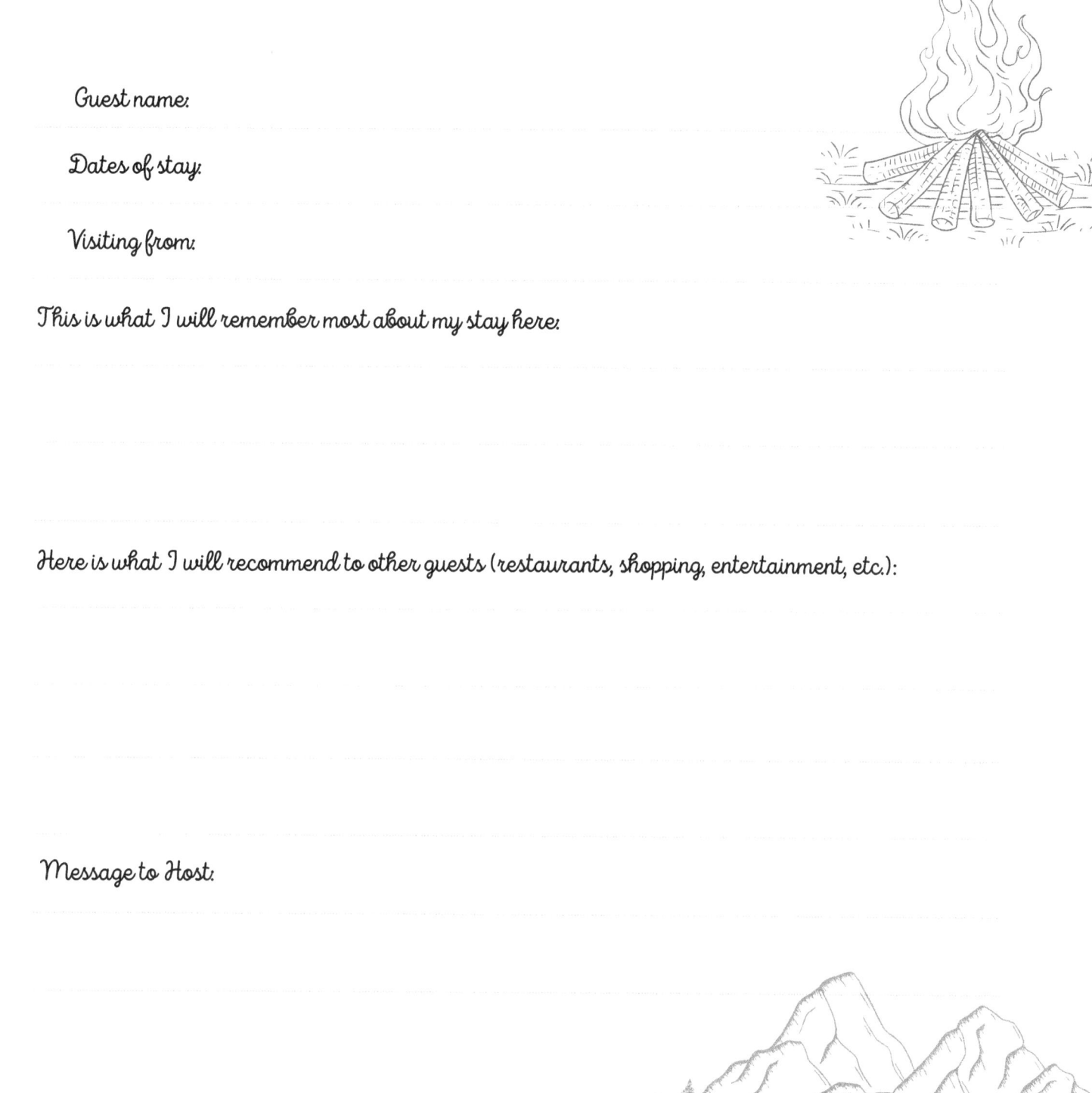

Guest name:

Dates of stay:

Visiting from:

This is what I will remember most about my stay here:

Here is what I will recommend to other guests (restaurants, shopping, entertainment, etc.):

Message to Host:

Guest name:

Dates of stay:

Visiting from:

This is what I will remember most about my stay here:

Here is what I will recommend to other guests (restaurants, shopping, entertainment, etc.):

Message to Host:

Guest name:

Dates of stay:

Visiting from:

This is what I will remember most about my stay here:

Here is what I will recommend to other guests (restaurants, shopping, entertainment, etc.):

Message to Host:

Guest name:

Dates of stay:

Visiting from:

This is what I will remember most about my stay here:

Here is what I will recommend to other guests (restaurants, shopping, entertainment, etc.):

Message to Host:

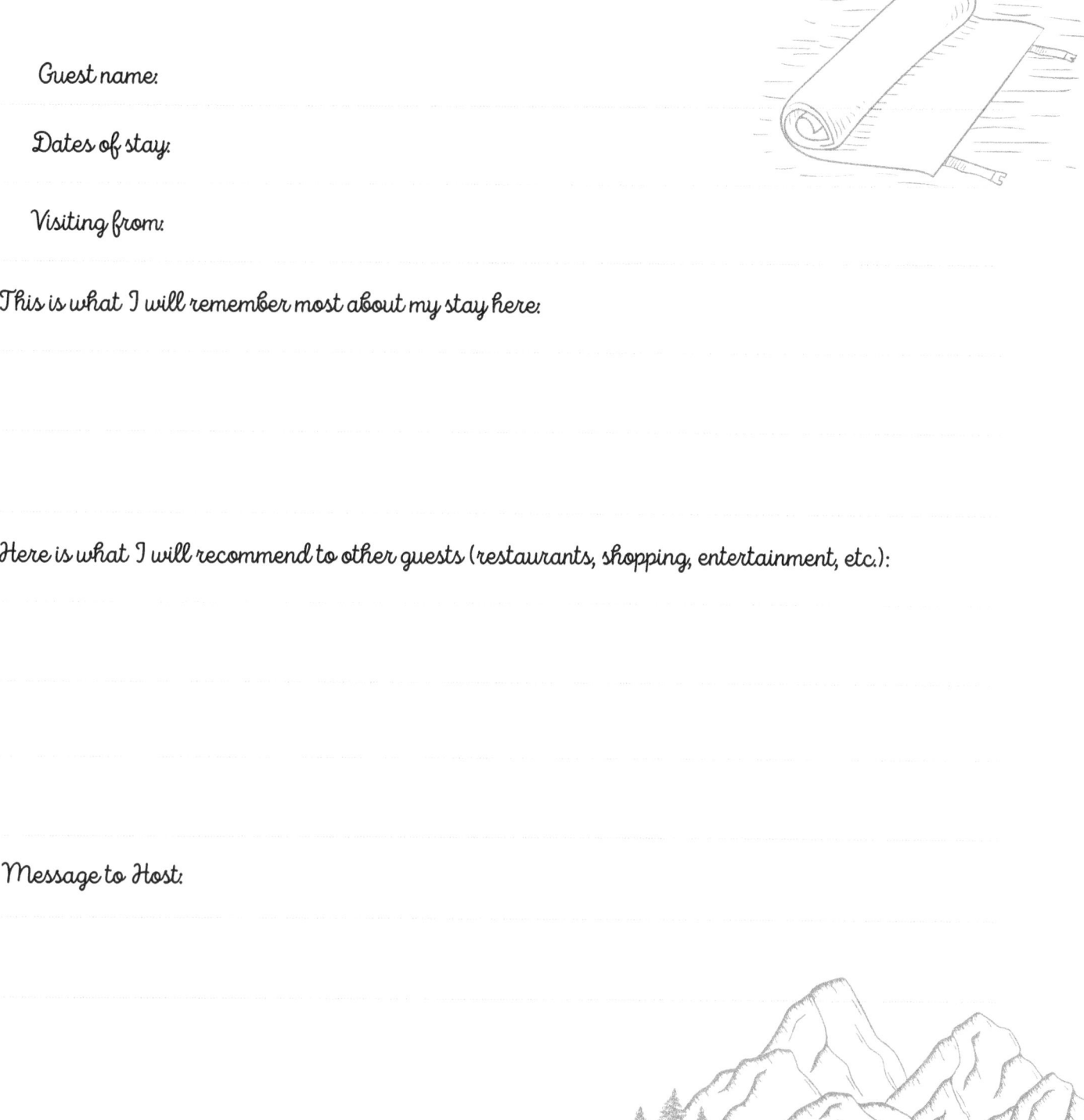

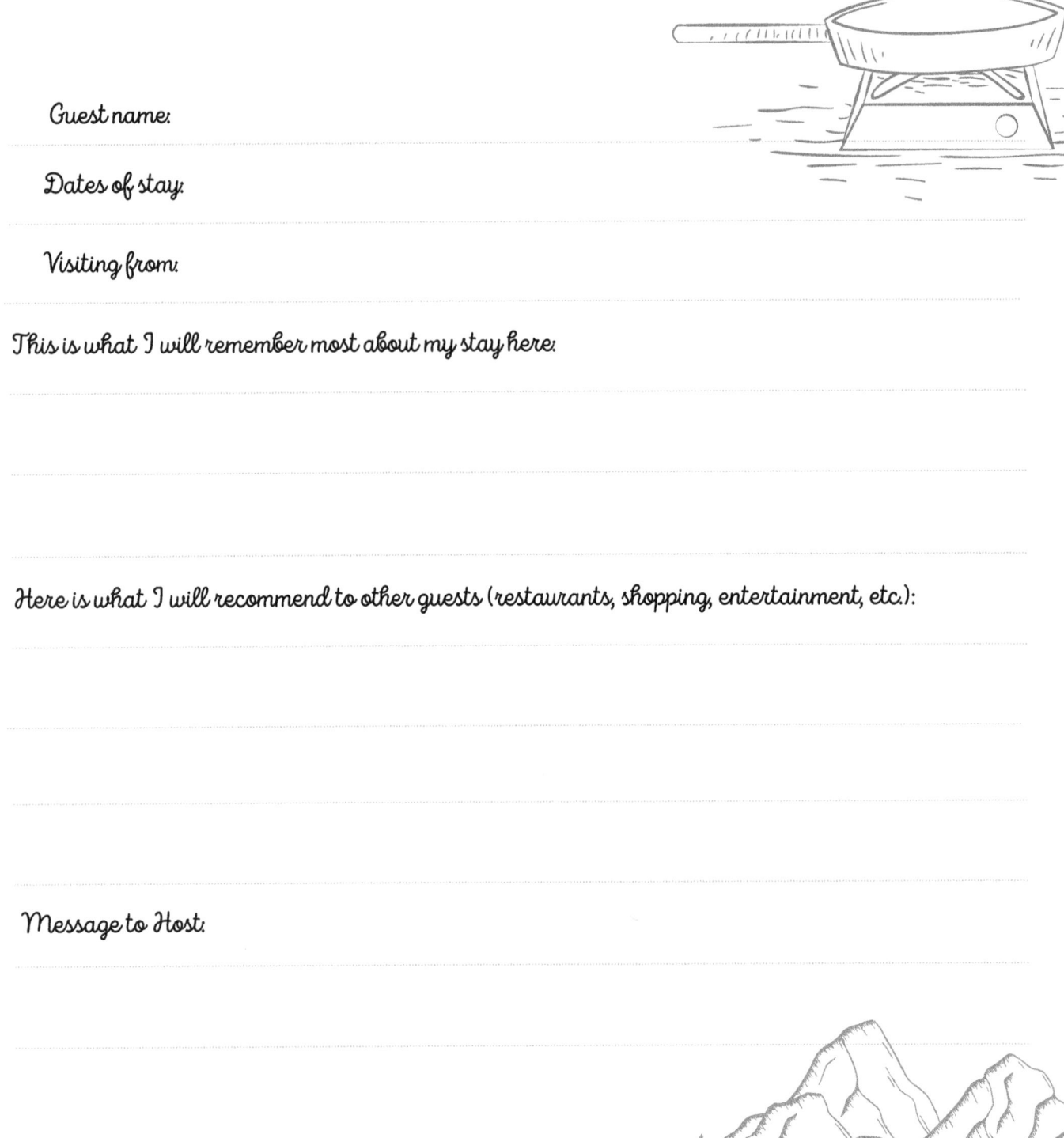

Guest name:

Dates of stay:

Visiting from:

This is what I will remember most about my stay here:

Here is what I will recommend to other guests (restaurants, shopping, entertainment, etc.):

Message to Host:

Guest name:

Dates of stay:

Visiting from:

This is what I will remember most about my stay here:

Here is what I will recommend to other guests (restaurants, shopping, entertainment, etc.):

Message to Host:

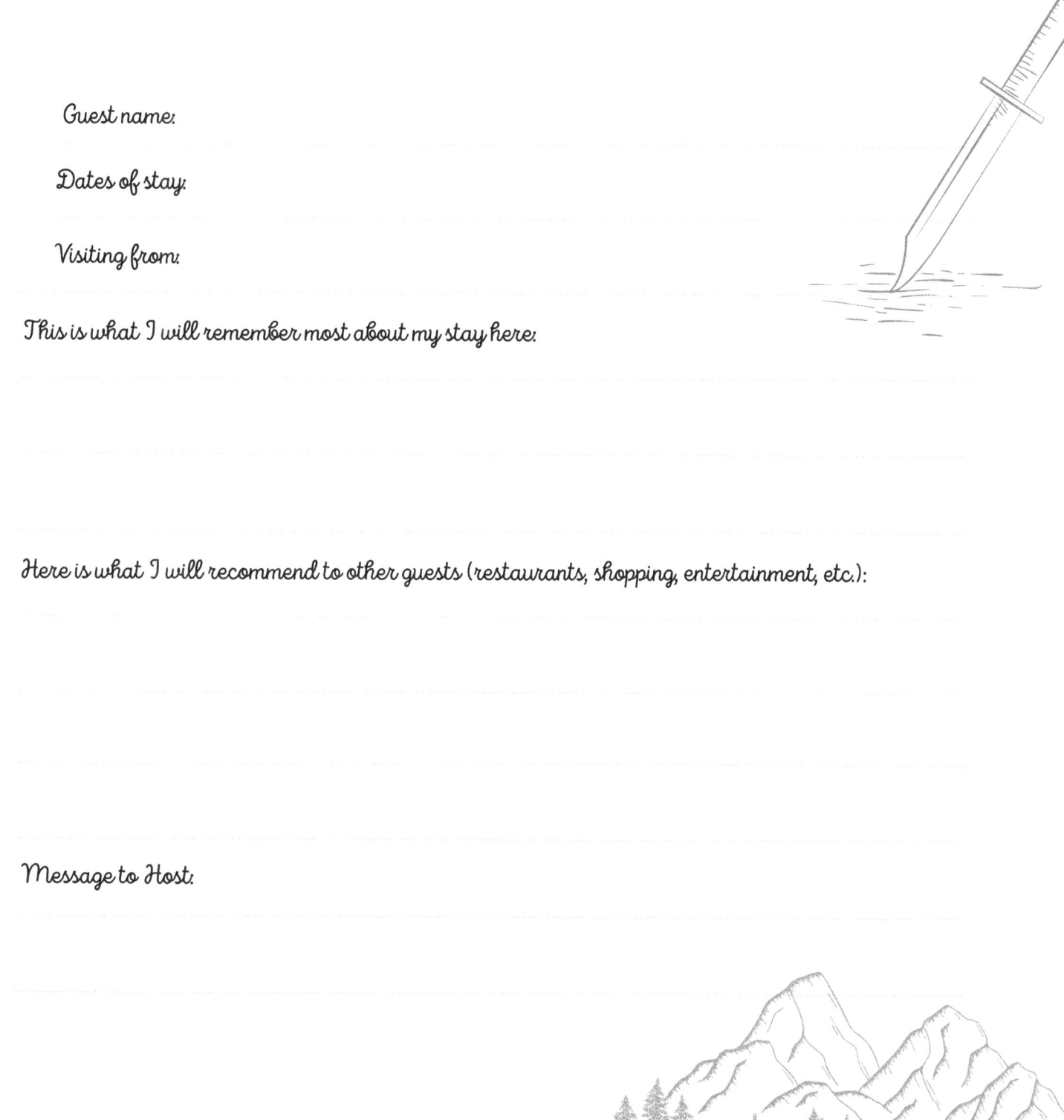

Guest name:

Dates of stay:

Visiting from:

This is what I will remember most about my stay here:

Here is what I will recommend to other guests (restaurants, shopping, entertainment, etc.):

Message to Host:

Guest name:

Dates of stay:

Visiting from:

This is what I will remember most about my stay here:

Here is what I will recommend to other guests (restaurants, shopping, entertainment, etc.):

Message to Host:

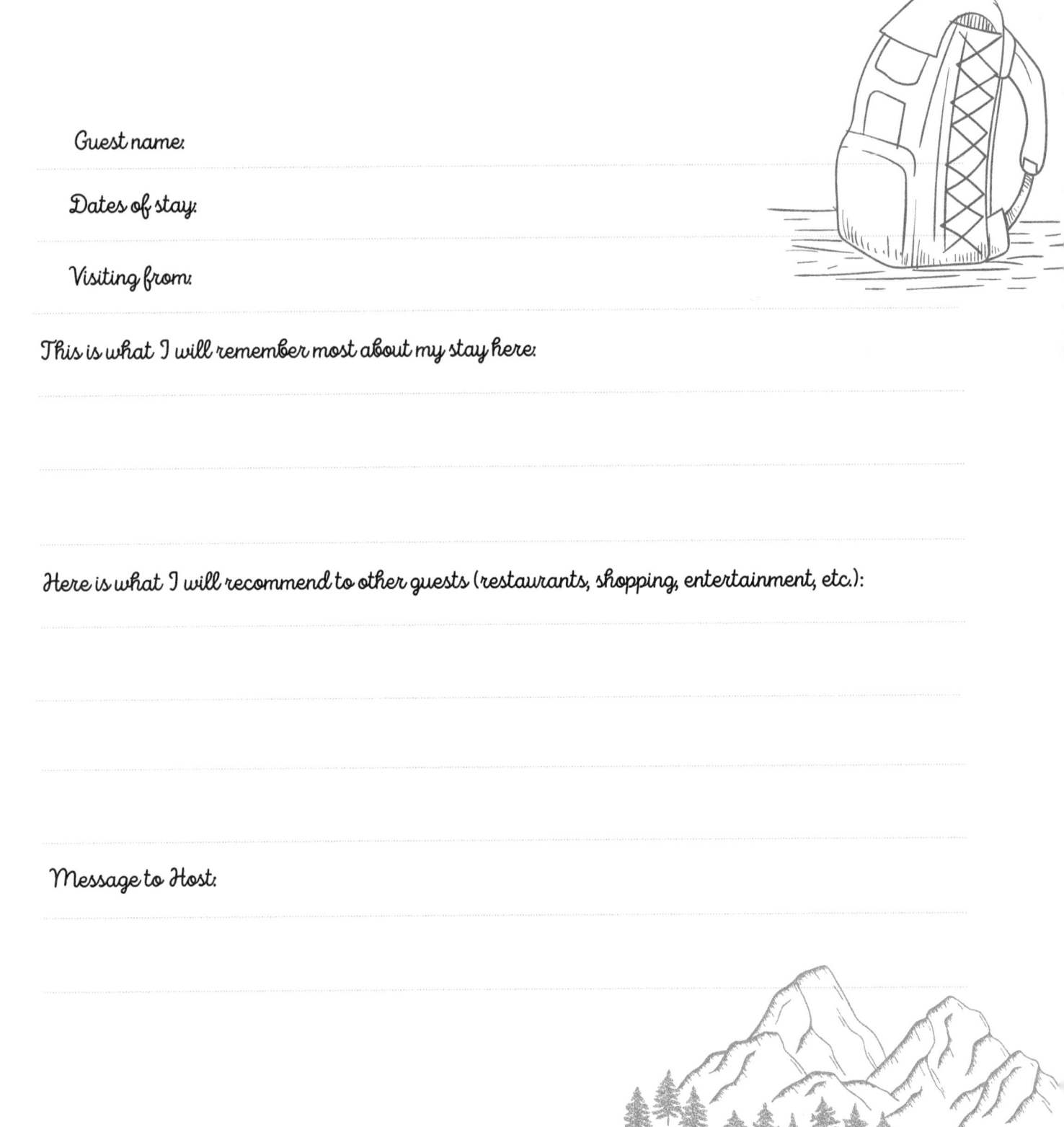

Guest name:

Dates of stay:

Visiting from:

This is what I will remember most about my stay here:

Here is what I will recommend to other guests (restaurants, shopping, entertainment, etc.):

Message to Host:

Guest name:

Dates of stay:

Visiting from:

This is what I will remember most about my stay here:

Here is what I will recommend to other guests (restaurants, shopping, entertainment, etc.):

Message to Host:

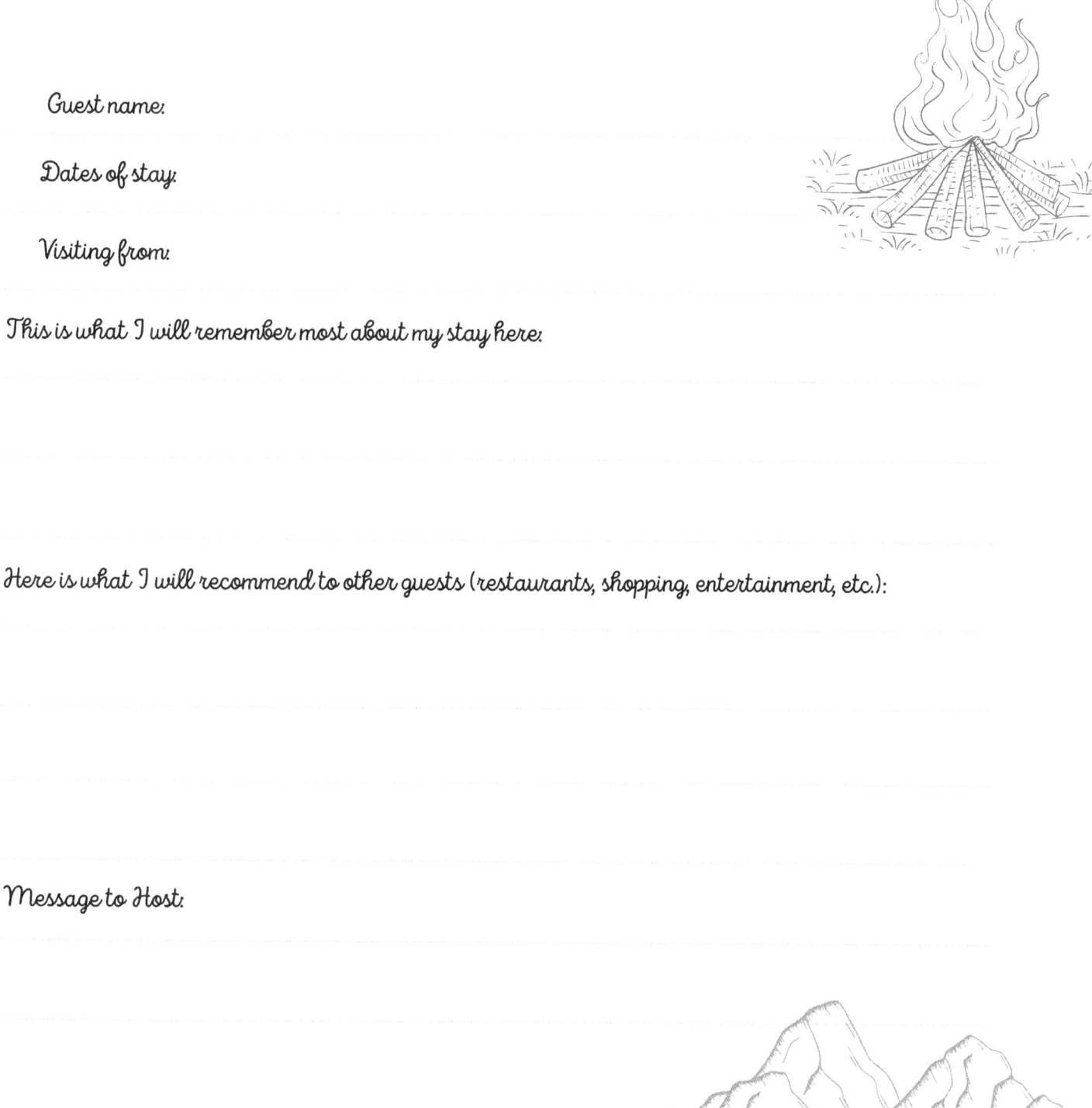

Guest name:

Dates of stay:

Visiting from:

This is what I will remember most about my stay here:

Here is what I will recommend to other guests (restaurants, shopping, entertainment, etc.):

Message to Host:

Guest name:

Dates of stay:

Visiting from:

This is what I will remember most about my stay here:

Here is what I will recommend to other guests (restaurants, shopping, entertainment, etc.):

Message to Host:

Guest name:

Dates of stay:

Visiting from:

This is what I will remember most about my stay here:

Here is what I will recommend to other guests (restaurants, shopping, entertainment, etc.):

Message to Host:

Guest name:

Dates of stay:

Visiting from:

This is what I will remember most about my stay here:

Here is what I will recommend to other guests (restaurants, shopping, entertainment, etc.):

Message to Host:

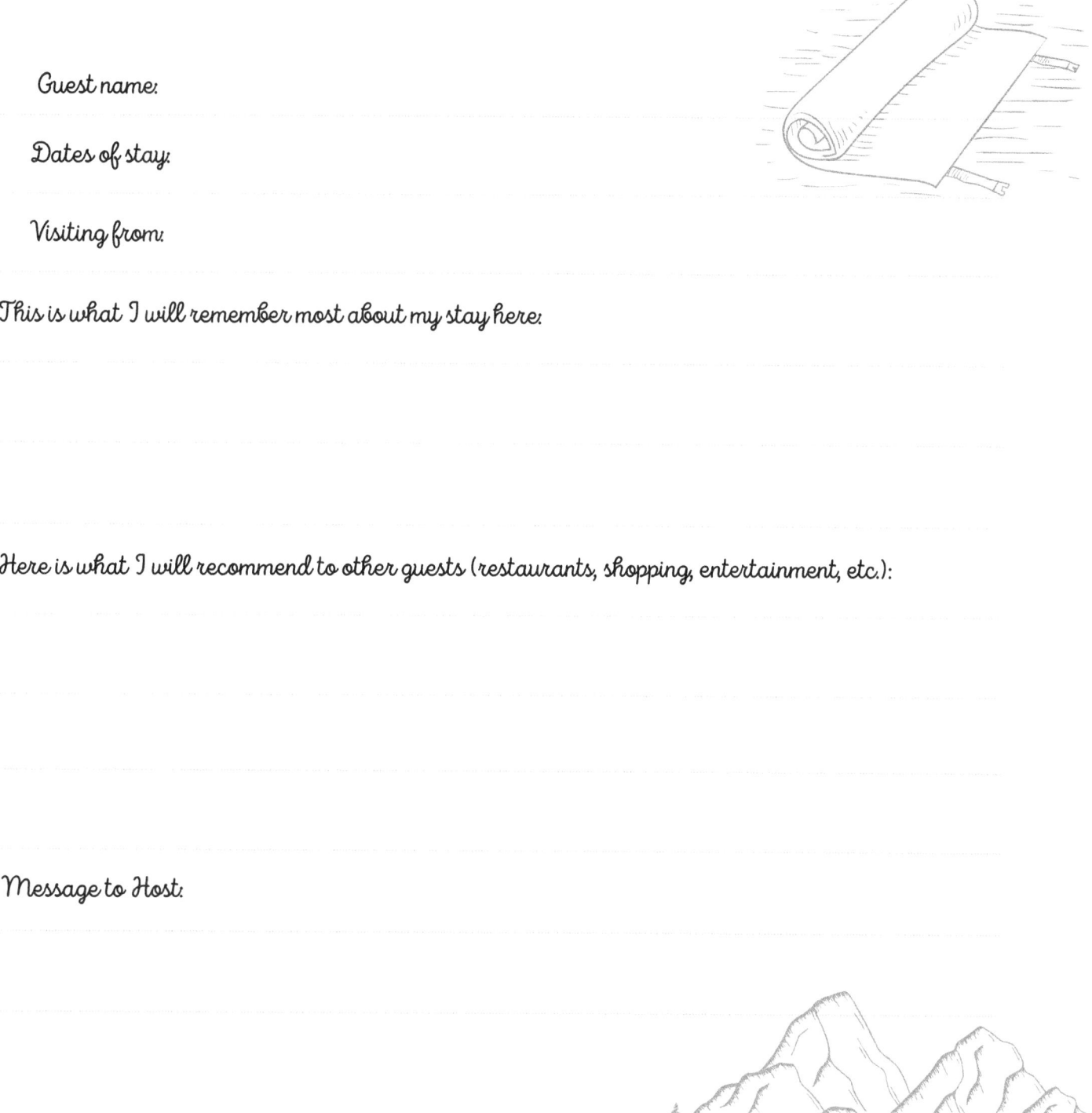

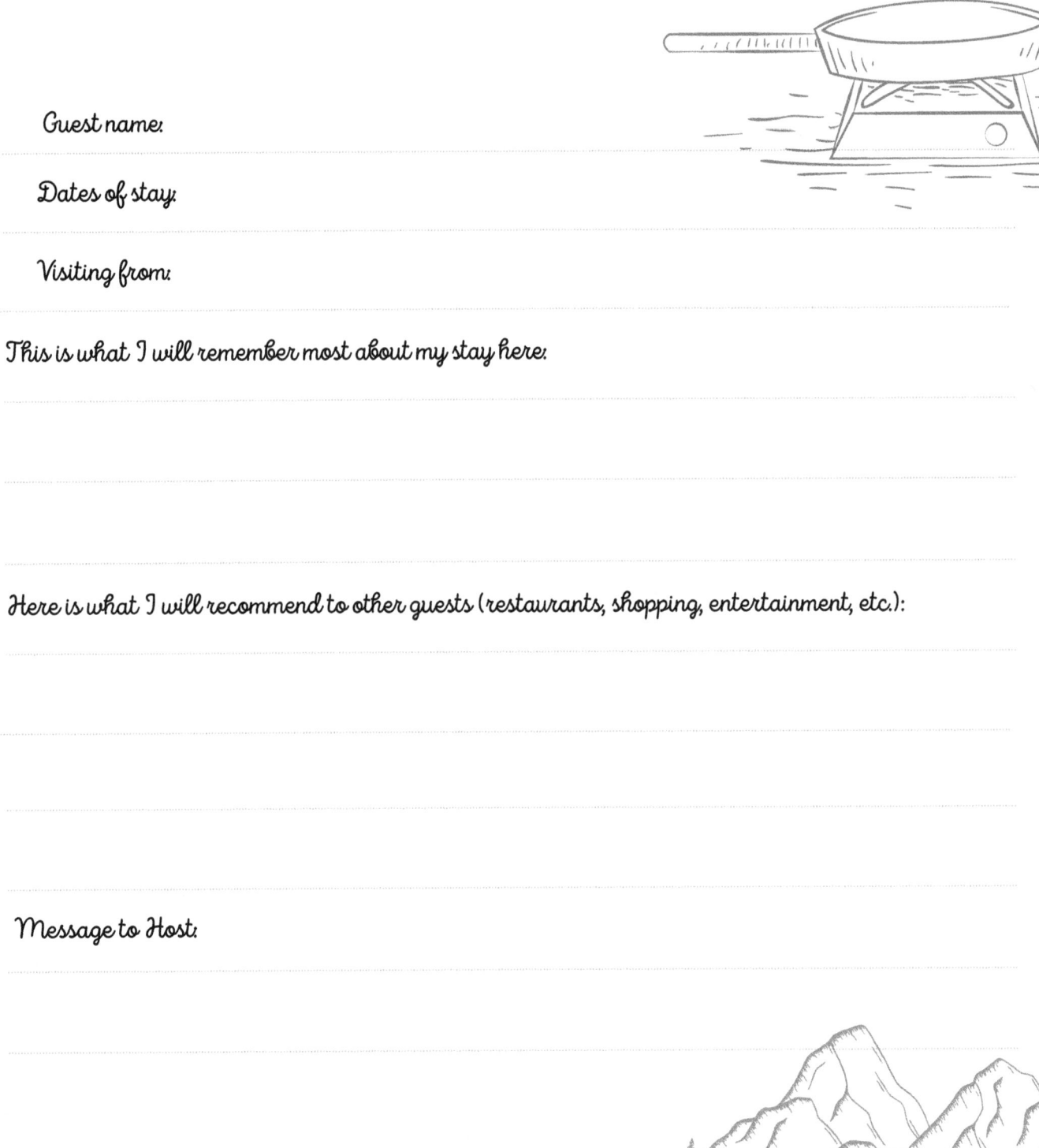

Guest name:

Dates of stay:

Visiting from:

This is what I will remember most about my stay here:

Here is what I will recommend to other guests (restaurants, shopping, entertainment, etc.):

Message to Host:

Guest name:

Dates of stay:

Visiting from:

This is what I will remember most about my stay here:

Here is what I will recommend to other guests (restaurants, shopping, entertainment, etc.):

Message to Host:

Guest name:

Dates of stay:

Visiting from:

This is what I will remember most about my stay here:

Here is what I will recommend to other guests (restaurants, shopping, entertainment, etc.):

Message to Host:

Guest name:

Dates of stay:

Visiting from:

This is what I will remember most about my stay here:

Here is what I will recommend to other guests (restaurants, shopping, entertainment, etc.):

Message to Host:

Guest name:

Dates of stay:

Visiting from:

This is what I will remember most about my stay here:

Here is what I will recommend to other guests (restaurants, shopping, entertainment, etc.):

Message to Host:

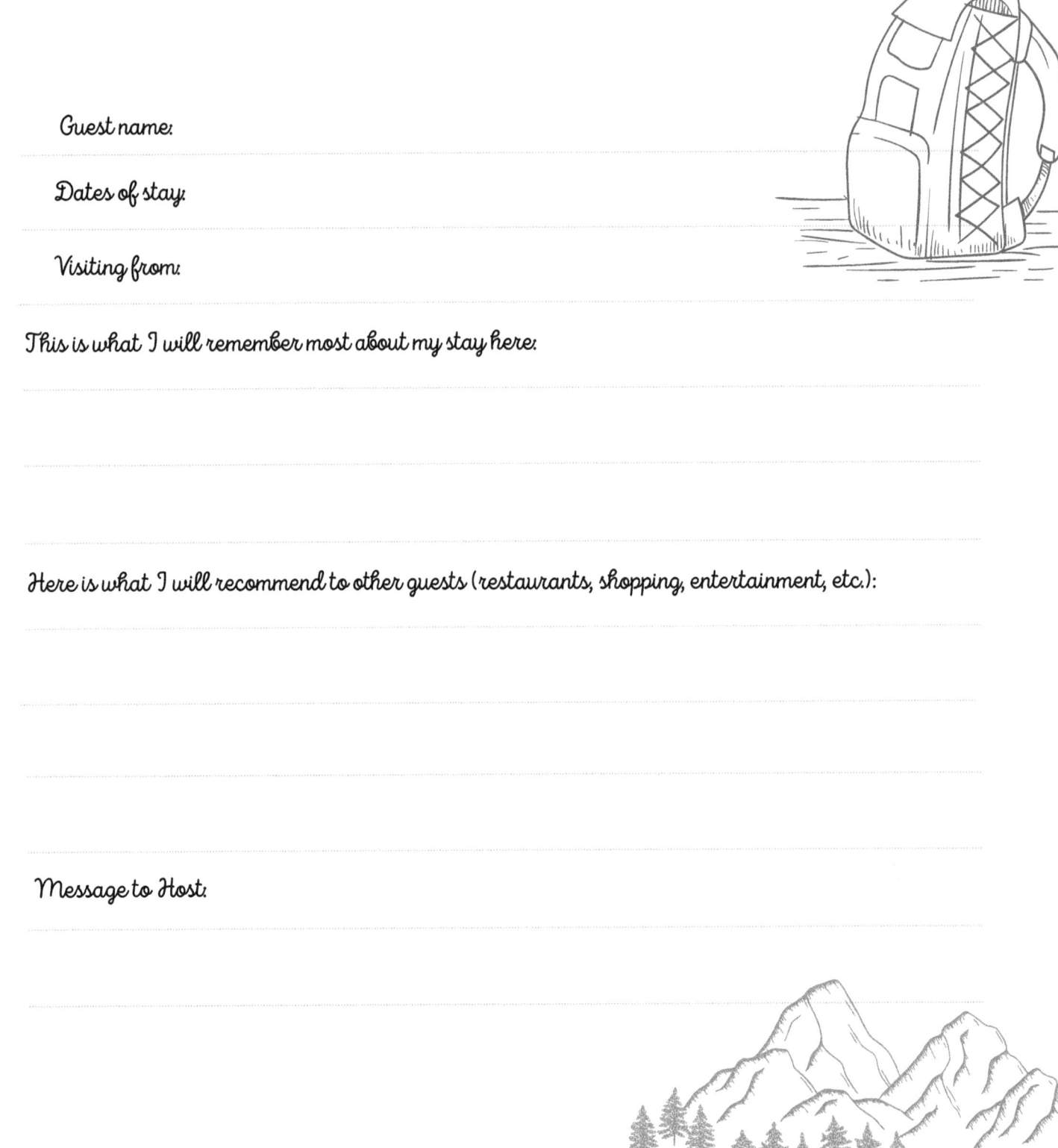

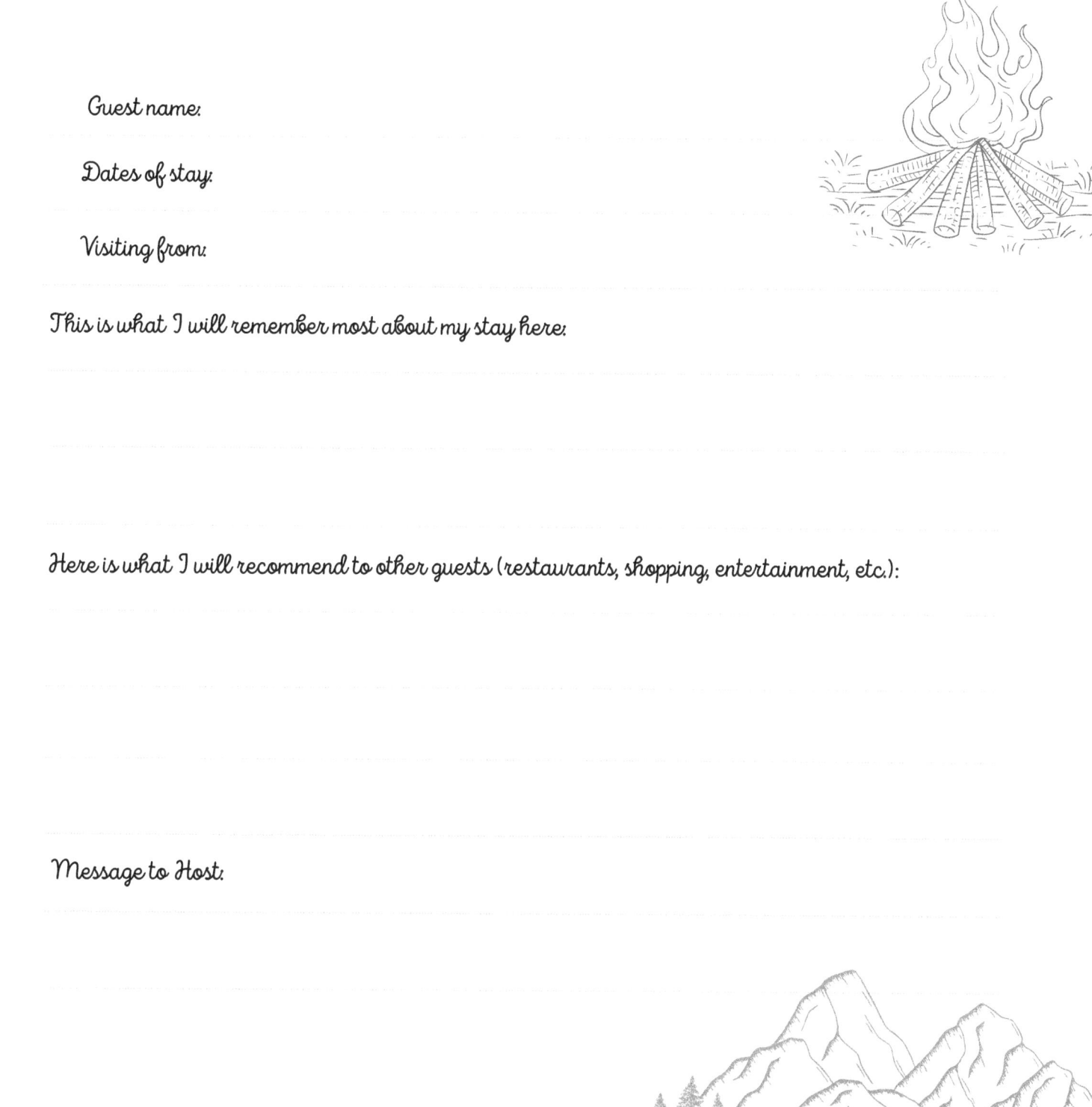

Guest name:

Dates of stay:

Visiting from:

This is what I will remember most about my stay here:

Here is what I will recommend to other guests (restaurants, shopping, entertainment, etc.):

Message to Host:

Guest name:

Dates of stay:

Visiting from:

This is what I will remember most about my stay here:

Here is what I will recommend to other guests (restaurants, shopping, entertainment, etc.):

Message to Host:

Guest name:

Dates of stay:

Visiting from:

This is what I will remember most about my stay here:

Here is what I will recommend to other guests (restaurants, shopping, entertainment, etc.):

Message to Host:

Guest name:

Dates of stay:

Visiting from:

This is what I will remember most about my stay here:

Here is what I will recommend to other guests (restaurants, shopping, entertainment, etc.):

Message to Host:

Guest name:

Dates of stay:

Visiting from:

This is what I will remember most about my stay here:

Here is what I will recommend to other guests (restaurants, shopping, entertainment, etc.):

Message to Host:

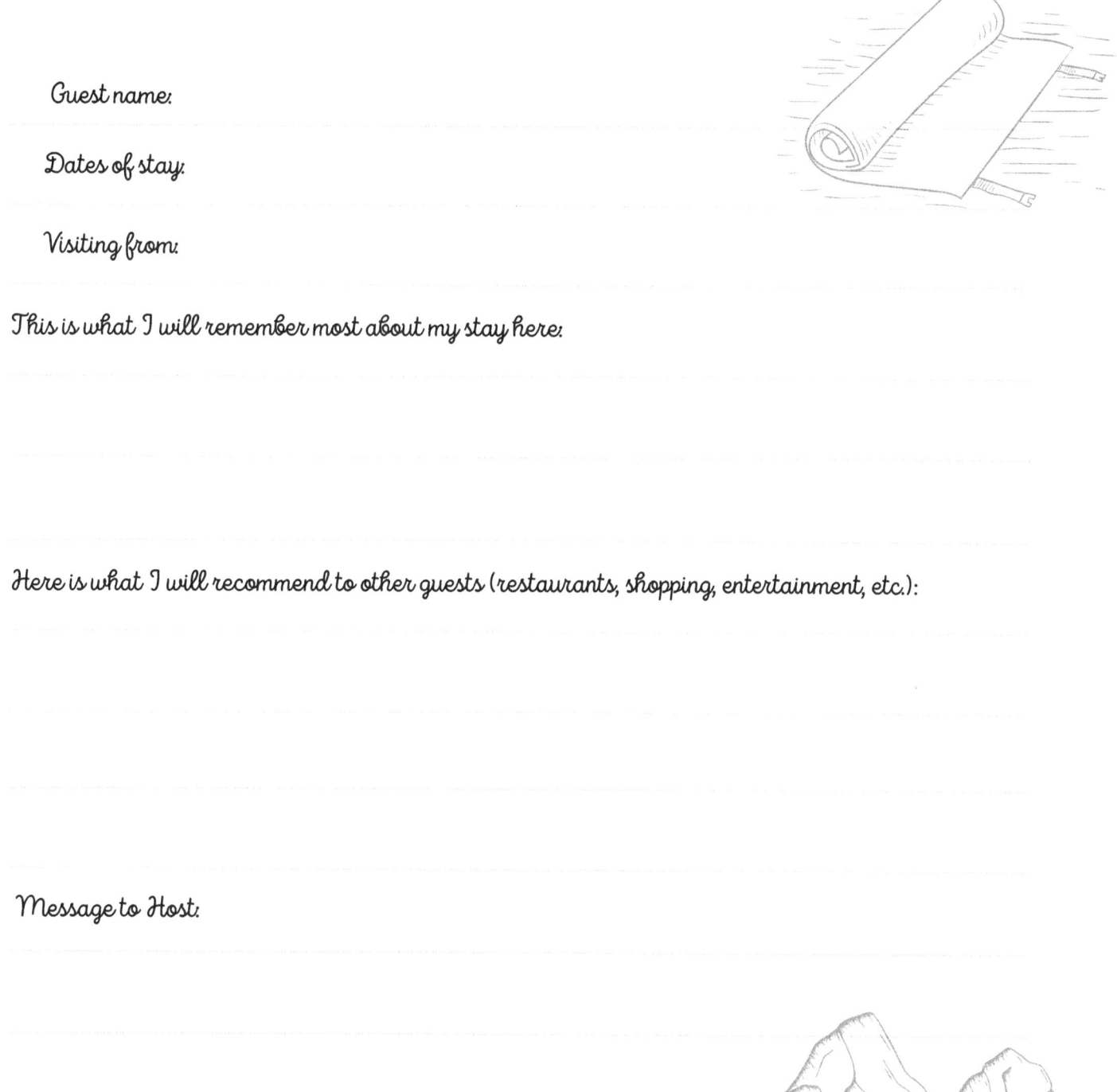

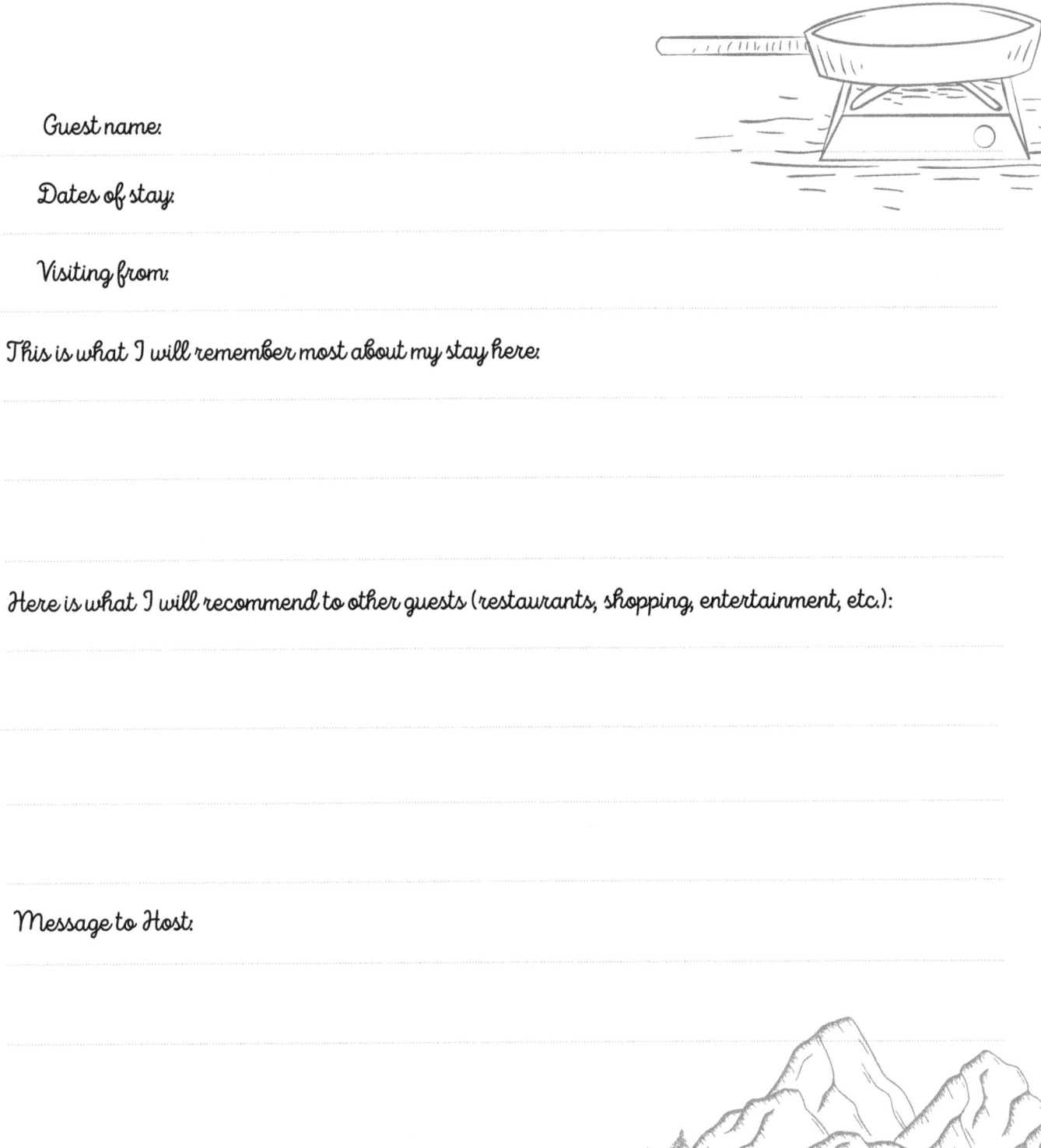

Guest name:

Dates of stay:

Visiting from:

This is what I will remember most about my stay here:

Here is what I will recommend to other guests (restaurants, shopping, entertainment, etc.):

Message to Host:

Guest name:

Dates of stay:

Visiting from:

This is what I will remember most about my stay here:

Here is what I will recommend to other guests (restaurants, shopping, entertainment, etc.):

Message to Host:

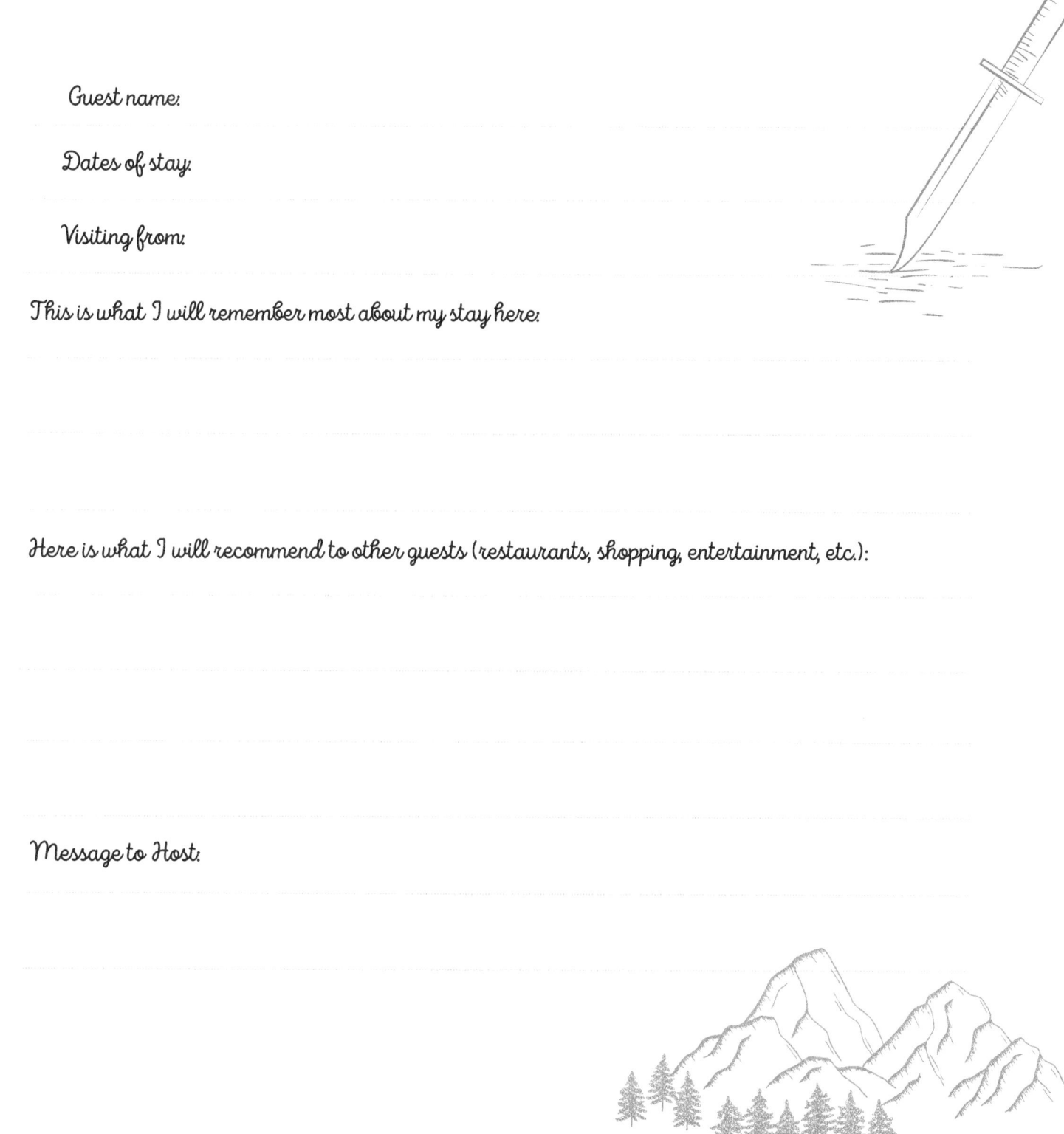

Guest name:

Dates of stay:

Visiting from:

This is what I will remember most about my stay here:

Here is what I will recommend to other guests (restaurants, shopping, entertainment, etc.):

Message to Host:

Guest name:

Dates of stay:

Visiting from:

This is what I will remember most about my stay here:

Here is what I will recommend to other guests (restaurants, shopping, entertainment, etc.):

Message to Host:

Guest name:

Dates of stay:

Visiting from:

This is what I will remember most about my stay here:

Here is what I will recommend to other guests (restaurants, shopping, entertainment, etc.):

Message to Host:

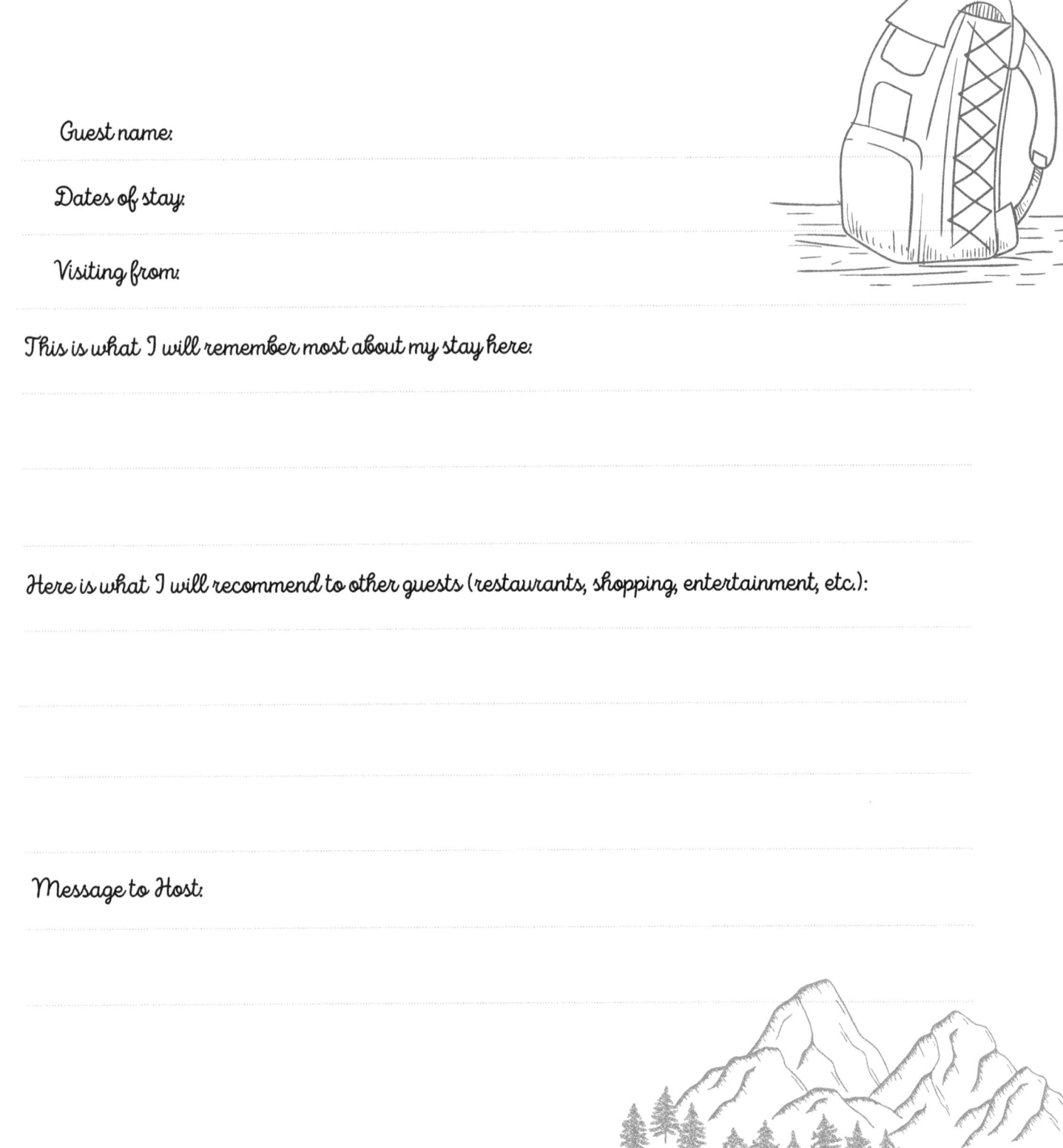

Guest name:

Dates of stay:

Visiting from:

This is what I will remember most about my stay here:

Here is what I will recommend to other guests (restaurants, shopping, entertainment, etc.):

Message to Host:

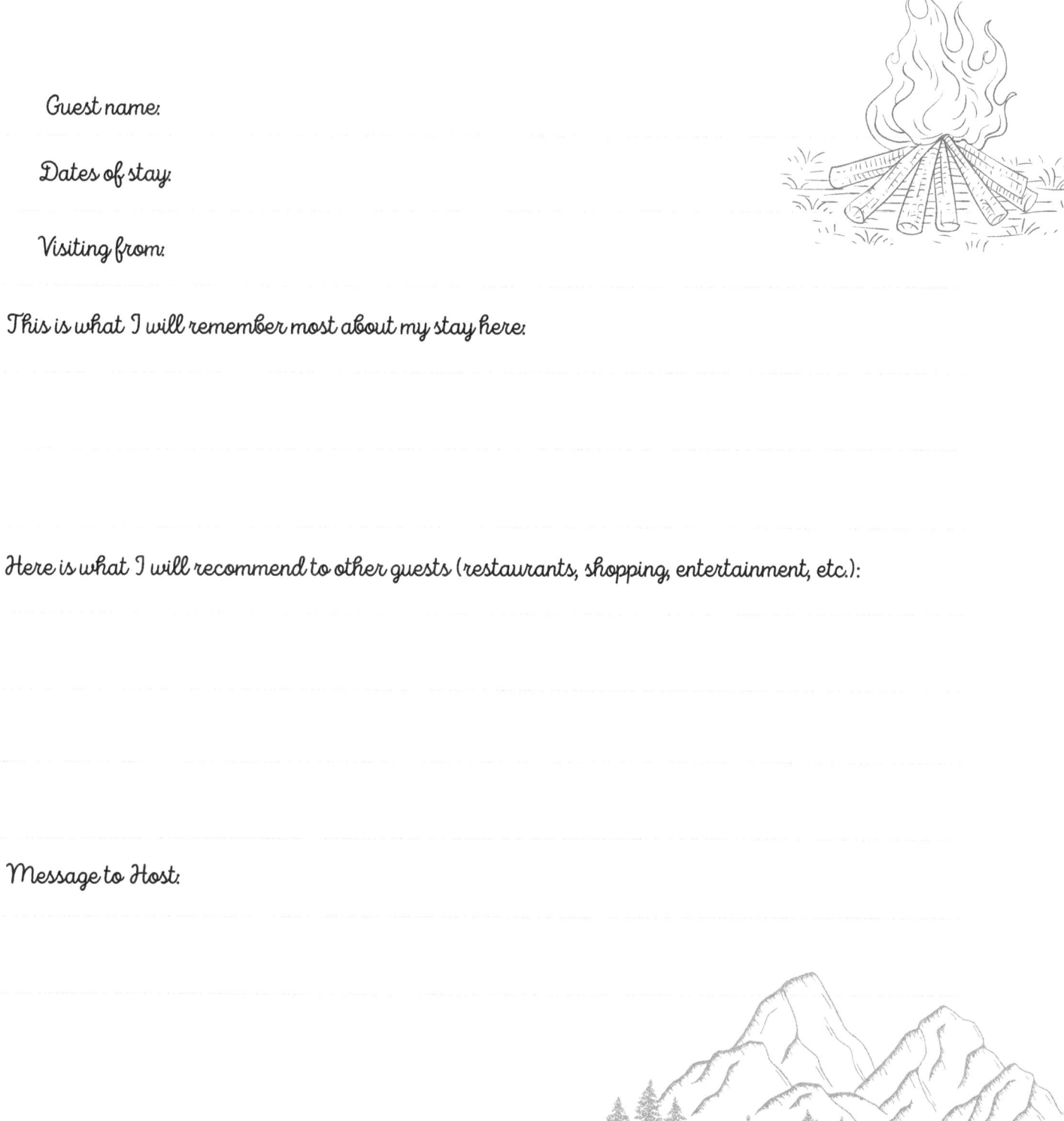

Guest name:

Dates of stay:

Visiting from:

This is what I will remember most about my stay here:

Here is what I will recommend to other guests (restaurants, shopping, entertainment, etc.):

Message to Host:

Guest name:

Dates of stay:

Visiting from:

This is what I will remember most about my stay here:

Here is what I will recommend to other guests (restaurants, shopping, entertainment, etc.):

Message to Host:

Guest name:

Dates of stay:

Visiting from:

This is what I will remember most about my stay here:

Here is what I will recommend to other guests (restaurants, shopping, entertainment, etc.):

Message to Host:

Guest name:

Dates of stay:

Visiting from:

This is what I will remember most about my stay here:

Here is what I will recommend to other guests (restaurants, shopping, entertainment, etc.):

Message to Host:

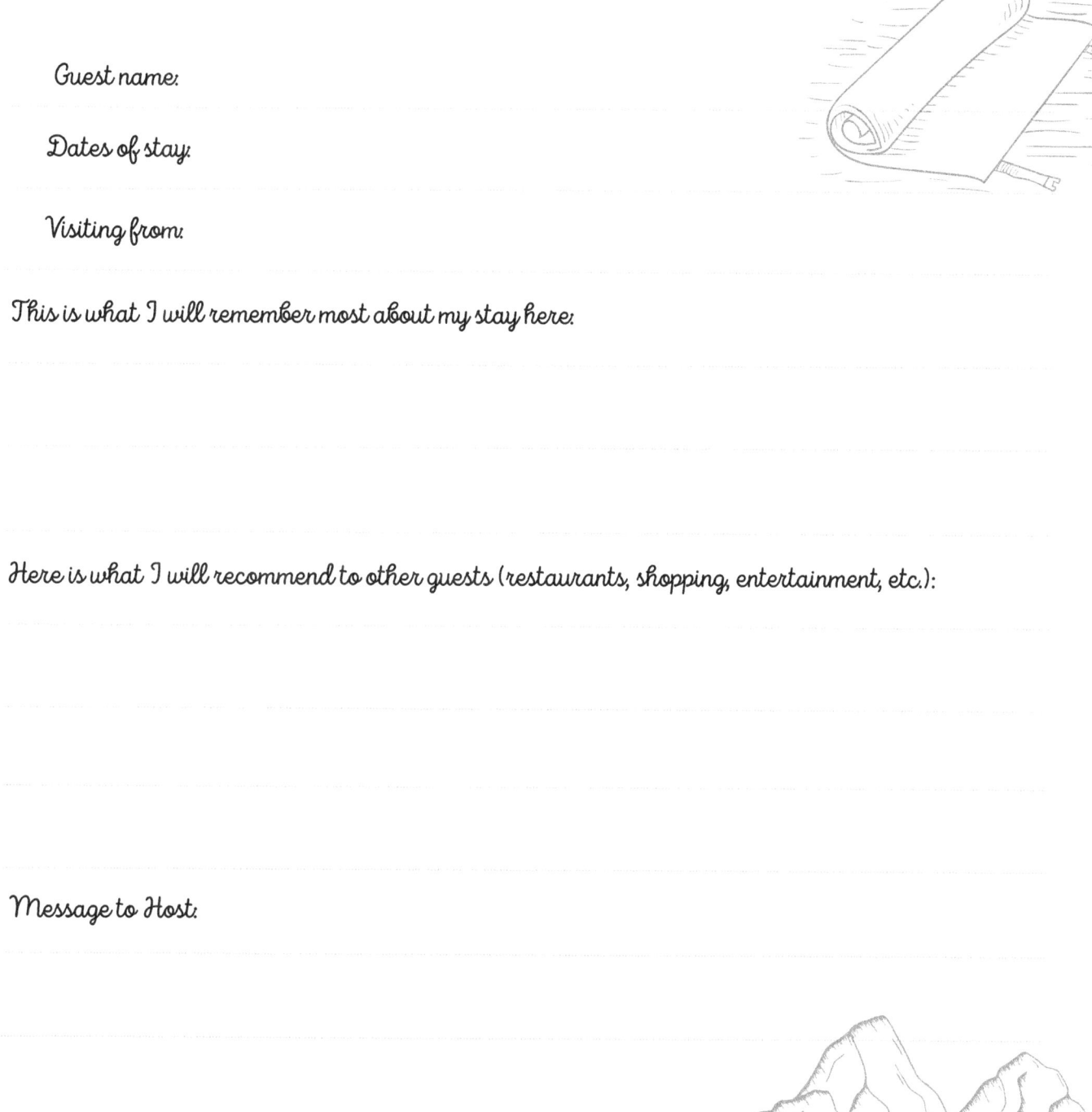

Guest name:

Dates of stay:

Visiting from:

This is what I will remember most about my stay here:

Here is what I will recommend to other guests (restaurants, shopping, entertainment, etc.):

Message to Host:

Guest name:

Dates of stay:

Visiting from:

This is what I will remember most about my stay here:

Here is what I will recommend to other guests (restaurants, shopping, entertainment, etc.):

Message to Host:

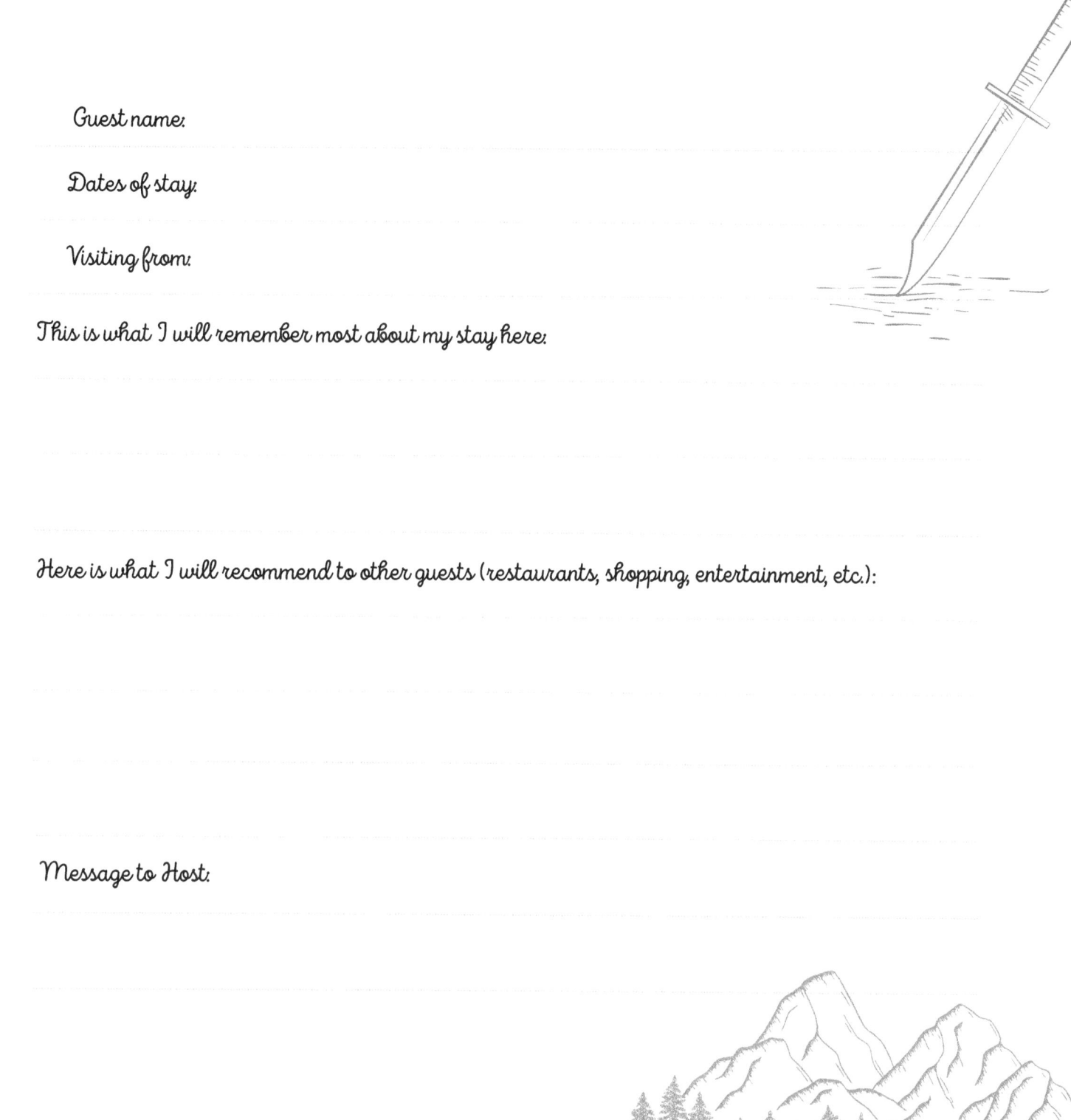

Guest name:

Dates of stay:

Visiting from:

This is what I will remember most about my stay here:

Here is what I will recommend to other guests (restaurants, shopping, entertainment, etc.):

Message to Host:

Guest name:

Dates of stay:

Visiting from:

This is what I will remember most about my stay here:

Here is what I will recommend to other guests (restaurants, shopping, entertainment, etc.):

Message to Host:

Guest name:

Dates of stay:

Visiting from:

This is what I will remember most about my stay here:

Here is what I will recommend to other guests (restaurants, shopping, entertainment, etc.):

Message to Host:

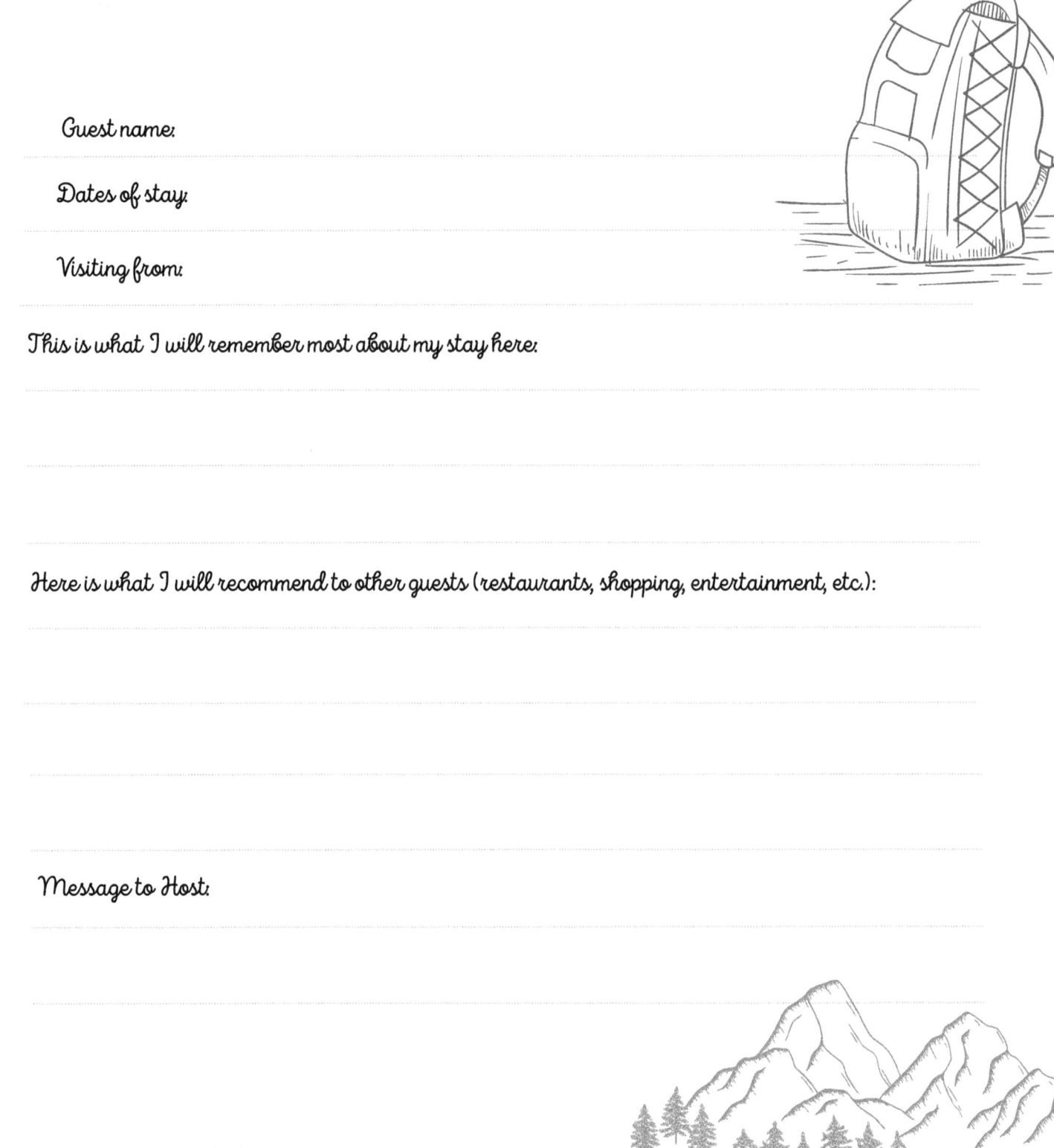

Guest name:

Dates of stay:

Visiting from:

This is what I will remember most about my stay here:

Here is what I will recommend to other guests (restaurants, shopping, entertainment, etc.):

Message to Host:

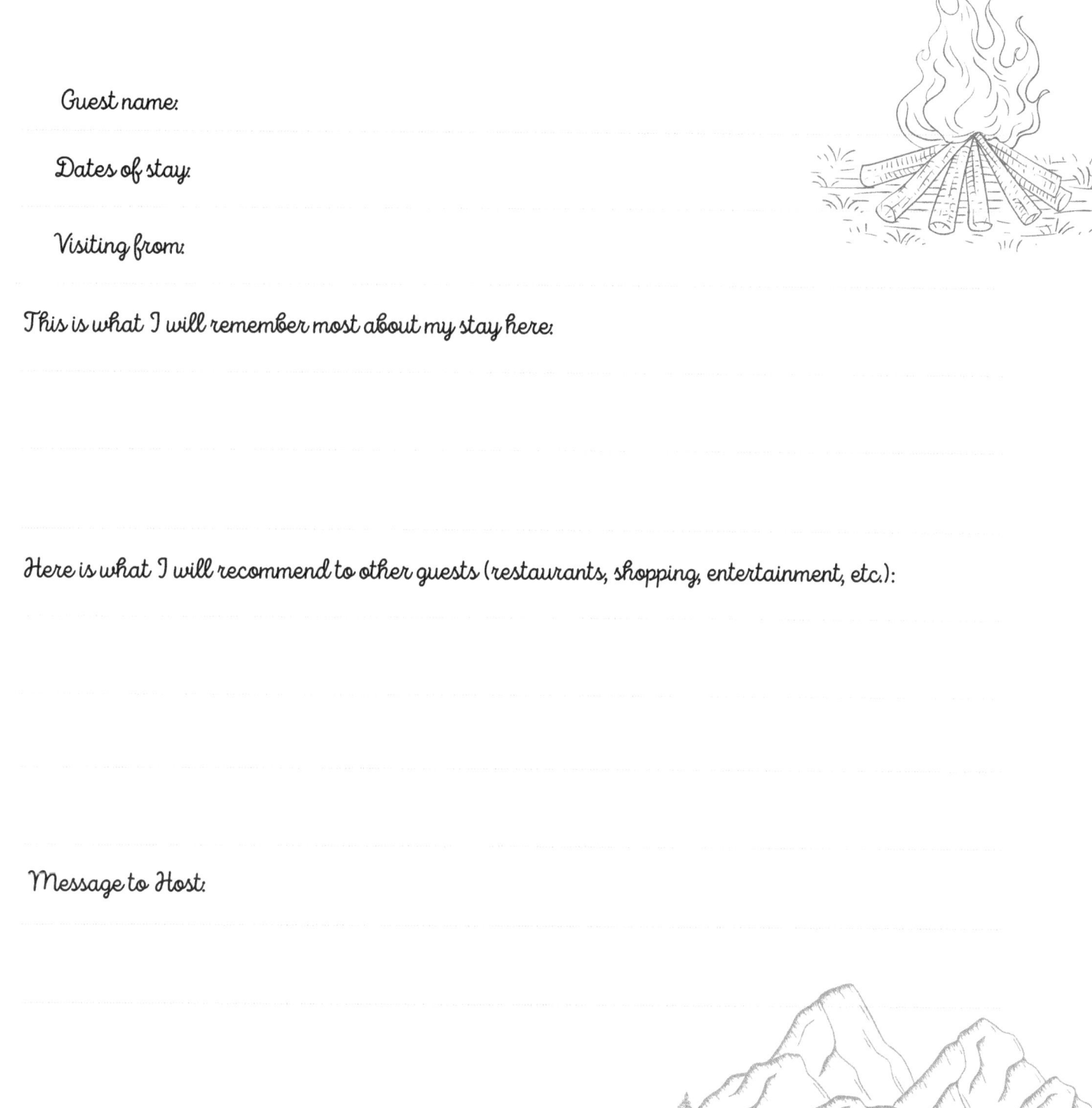

Guest name:

Dates of stay:

Visiting from:

This is what I will remember most about my stay here:

Here is what I will recommend to other guests (restaurants, shopping, entertainment, etc.):

Message to Host:

Guest name:

Dates of stay:

Visiting from:

This is what I will remember most about my stay here:

Here is what I will recommend to other guests (restaurants, shopping, entertainment, etc.):

Message to Host:

Guest name:

Dates of stay:

Visiting from:

This is what I will remember most about my stay here:

Here is what I will recommend to other guests (restaurants, shopping, entertainment, etc.):

Message to Host:

Guest name:

Dates of stay:

Visiting from:

This is what I will remember most about my stay here:

Here is what I will recommend to other guests (restaurants, shopping, entertainment, etc.):

Message to Host:

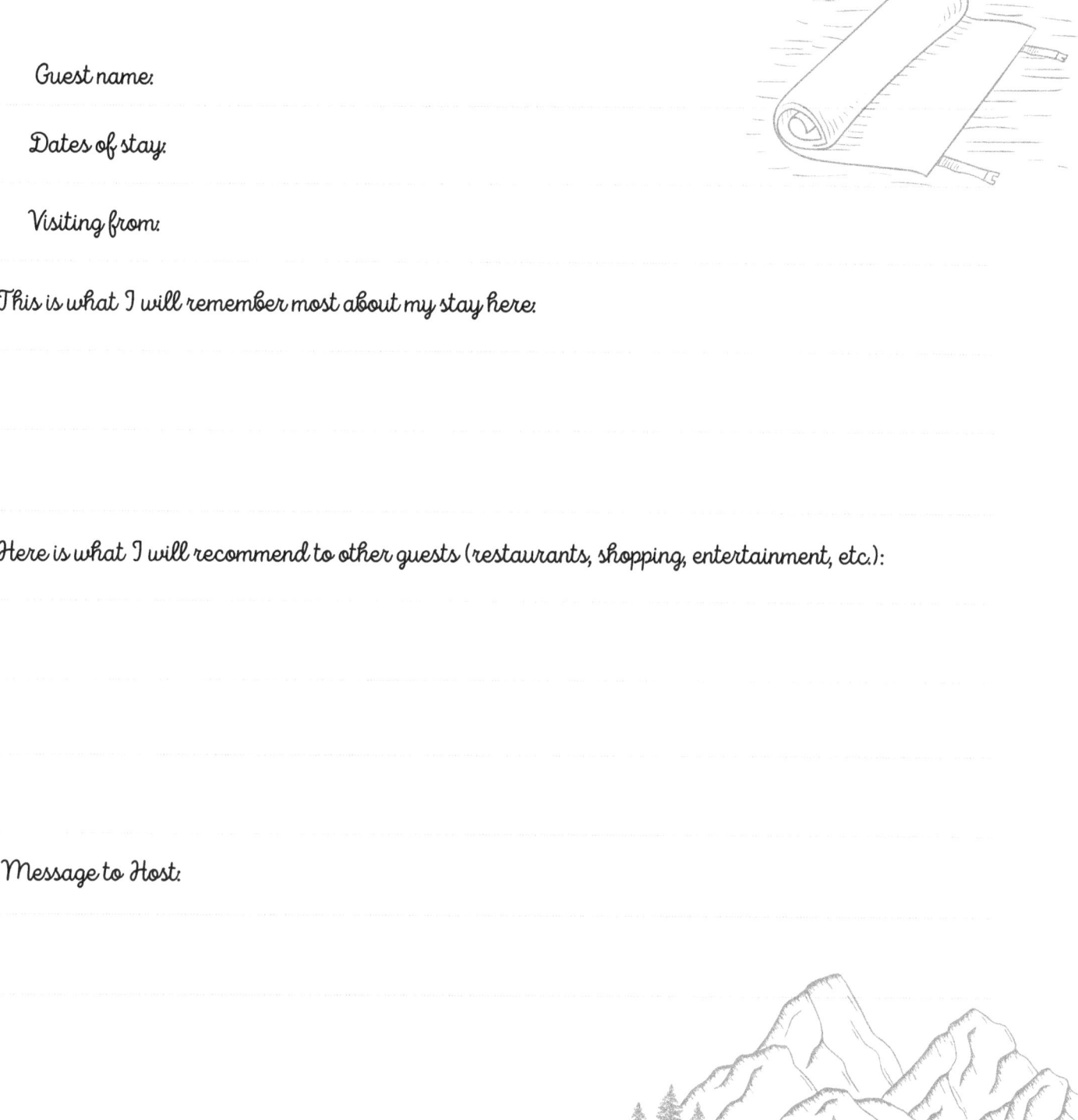

Guest name:

Dates of stay:

Visiting from:

This is what I will remember most about my stay here:

Here is what I will recommend to other guests (restaurants, shopping, entertainment, etc.):

Message to Host:

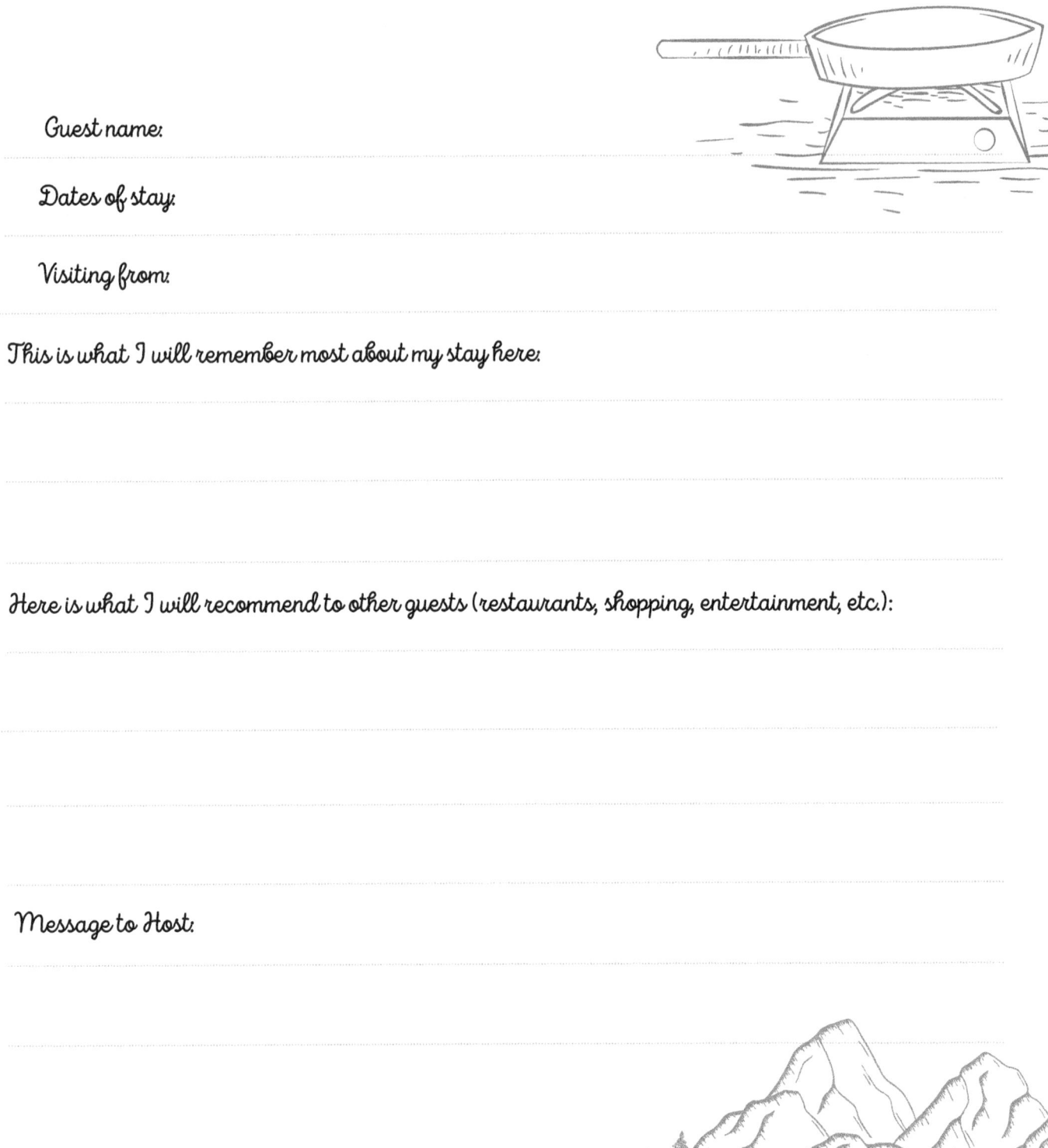

Guest name:

Dates of stay:

Visiting from:

This is what I will remember most about my stay here:

Here is what I will recommend to other guests (restaurants, shopping, entertainment, etc.):

Message to Host:

Guest name:

Dates of stay:

Visiting from:

This is what I will remember most about my stay here:

Here is what I will recommend to other guests (restaurants, shopping, entertainment, etc.):

Message to Host:

Guest name:

Dates of stay:

Visiting from:

This is what I will remember most about my stay here:

Here is what I will recommend to other guests (restaurants, shopping, entertainment, etc.):

Message to Host:

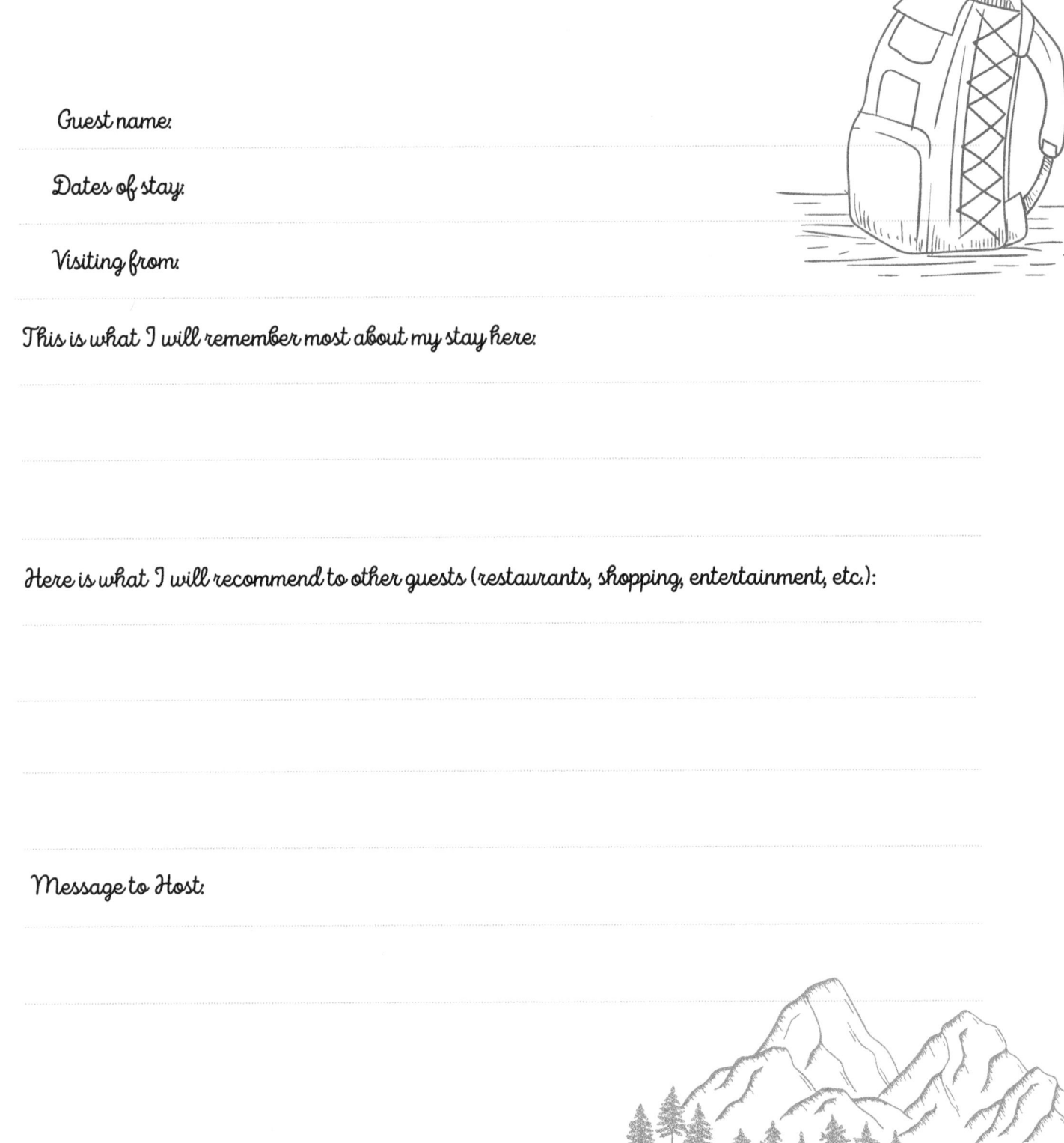

Guest name:

Dates of stay:

Visiting from:

This is what I will remember most about my stay here:

Here is what I will recommend to other guests (restaurants, shopping, entertainment, etc.):

Message to Host:

Guest name:

Dates of stay:

Visiting from:

This is what I will remember most about my stay here:

Here is what I will recommend to other guests (restaurants, shopping, entertainment, etc.):

Message to Host:

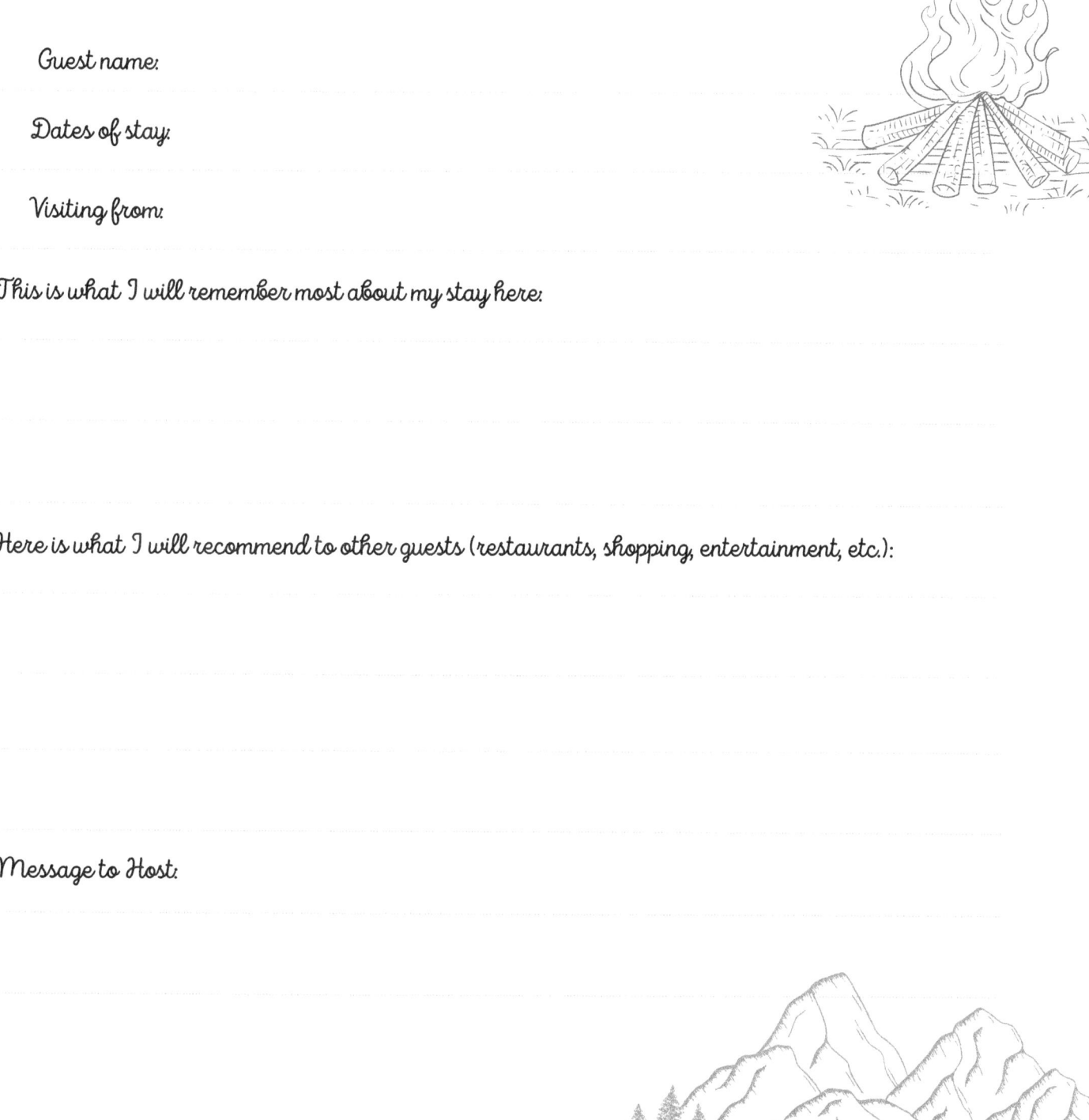

Guest name:

Dates of stay:

Visiting from:

This is what I will remember most about my stay here:

Here is what I will recommend to other guests (restaurants, shopping, entertainment, etc.):

Message to Host:

Guest name:

Dates of stay:

Visiting from:

This is what I will remember most about my stay here:

Here is what I will recommend to other guests (restaurants, shopping, entertainment, etc.):

Message to Host:

Guest name:

Dates of stay:

Visiting from:

This is what I will remember most about my stay here:

Here is what I will recommend to other guests (restaurants, shopping, entertainment, etc.):

Message to Host:

Guest name:

Dates of stay:

Visiting from:

This is what I will remember most about my stay here:

Here is what I will recommend to other guests (restaurants, shopping, entertainment, etc.):

Message to Host:

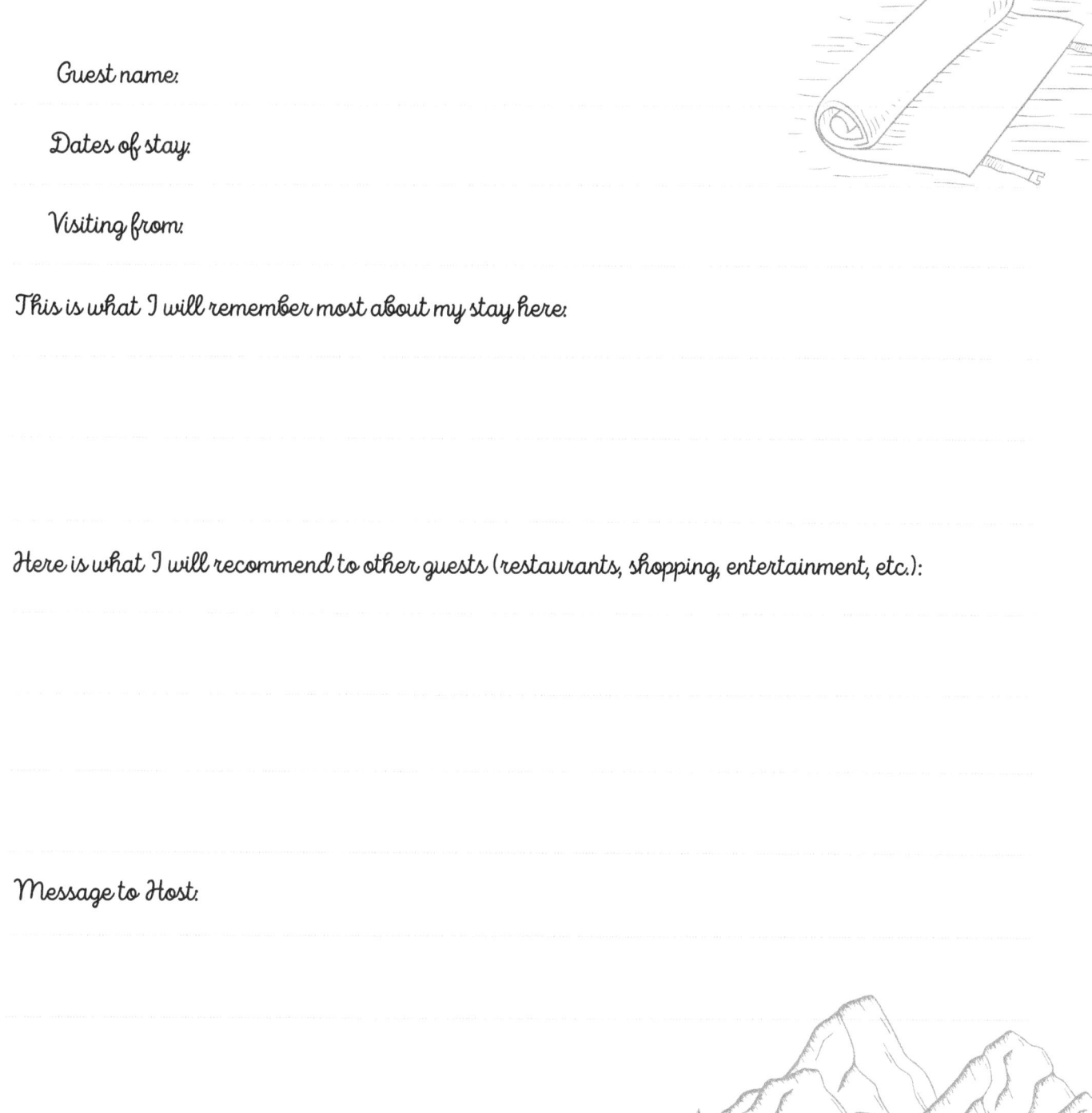

Guest name:

Dates of stay:

Visiting from:

This is what I will remember most about my stay here:

Here is what I will recommend to other guests (restaurants, shopping, entertainment, etc.):

Message to Host:

Guest name:

Dates of stay:

Visiting from:

This is what I will remember most about my stay here:

Here is what I will recommend to other guests (restaurants, shopping, entertainment, etc.):

Message to Host:

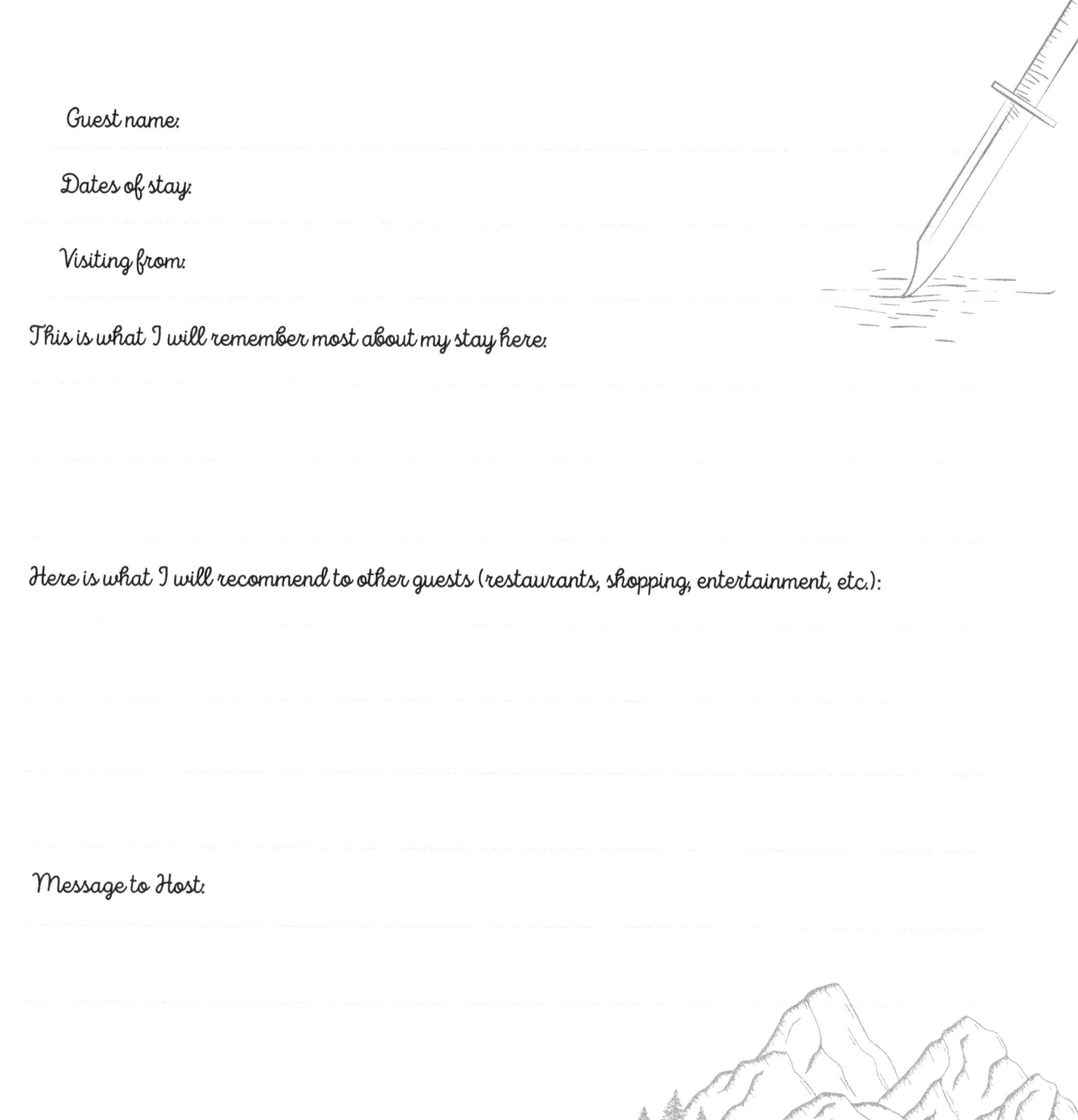

Guest name:

Dates of stay:

Visiting from:

This is what I will remember most about my stay here:

Here is what I will recommend to other guests (restaurants, shopping, entertainment, etc.):

Message to Host:

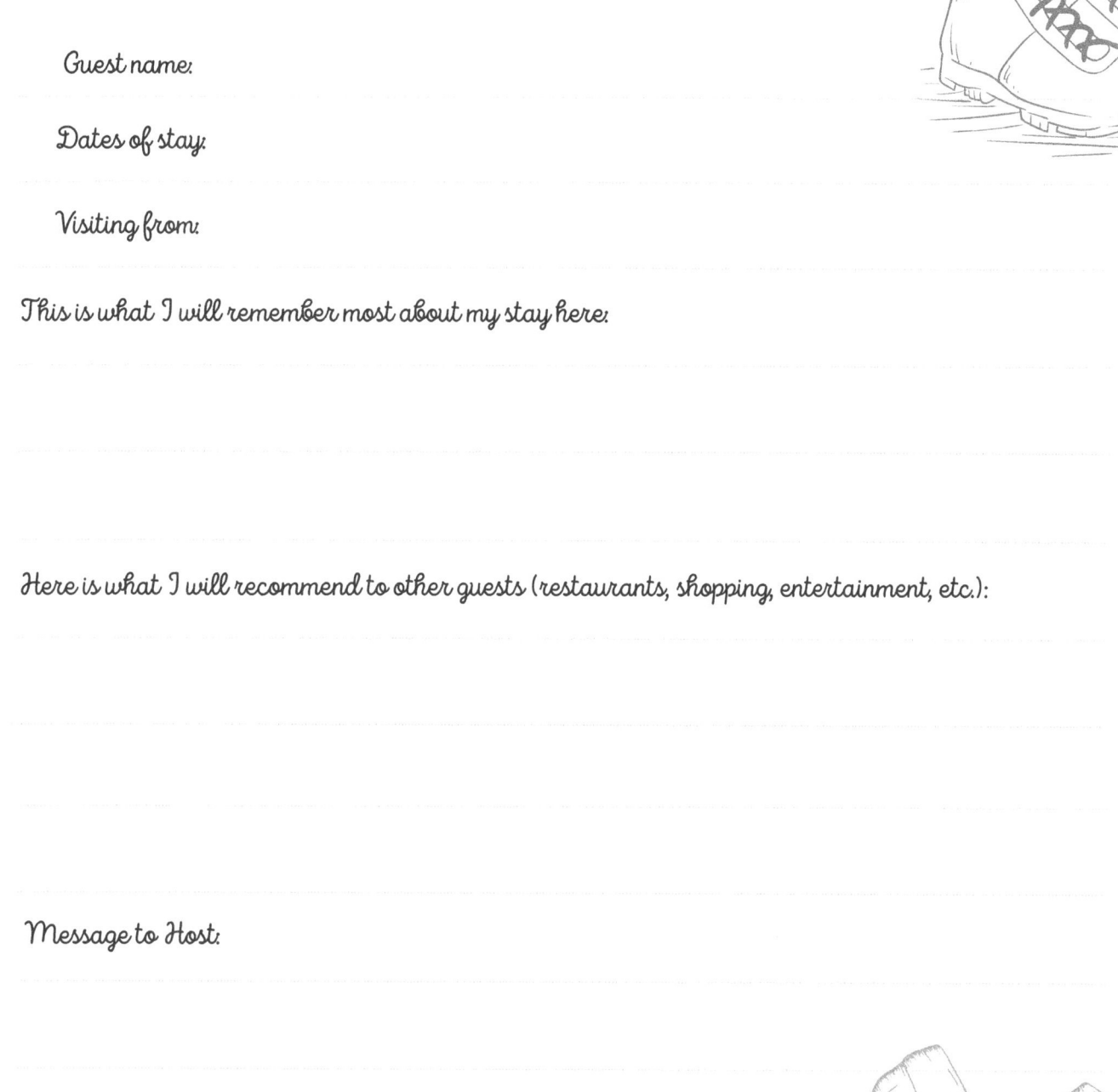

Guest name:

Dates of stay:

Visiting from:

This is what I will remember most about my stay here:

Here is what I will recommend to other guests (restaurants, shopping, entertainment, etc.):

Message to Host:

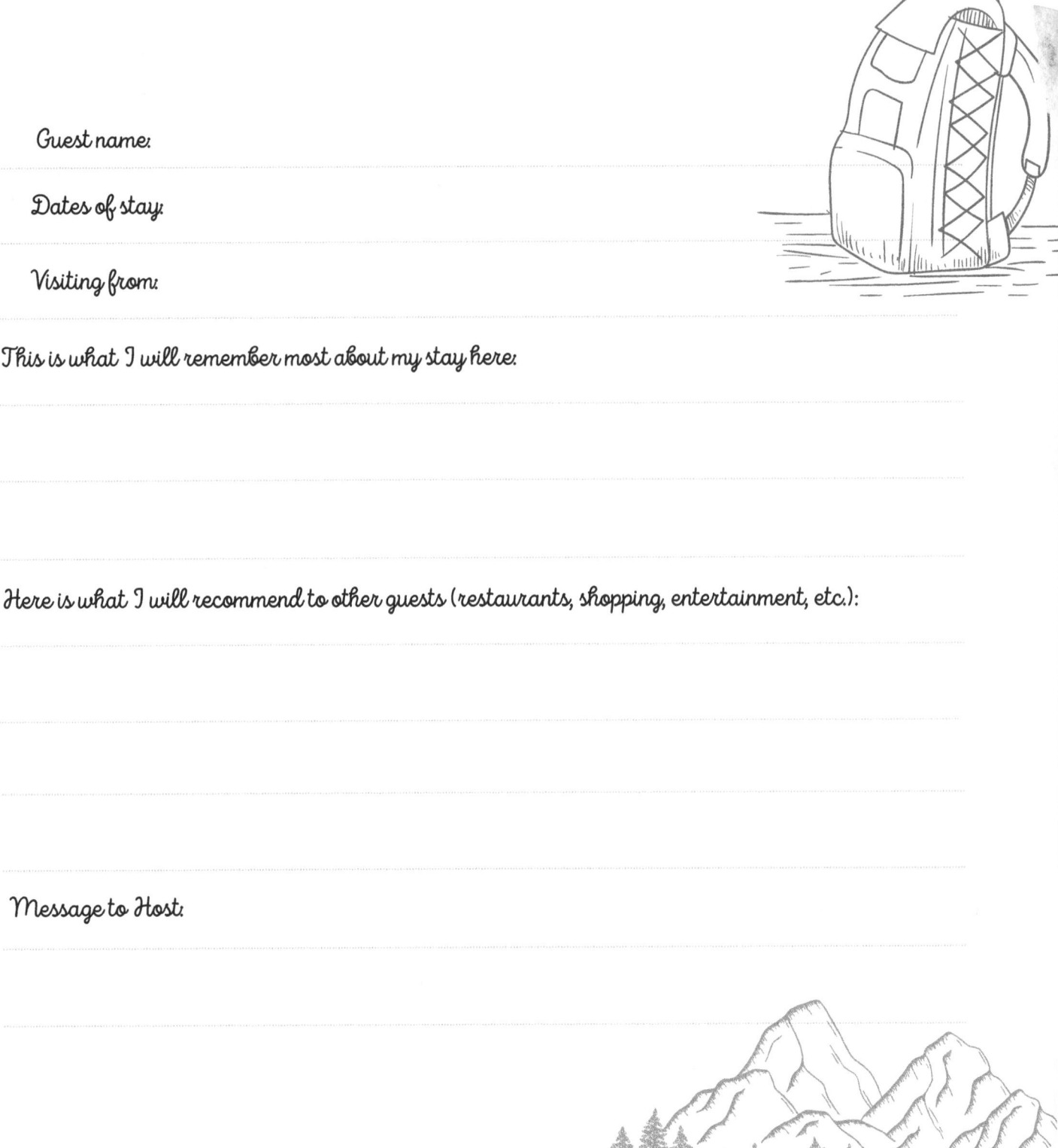

Guest name:

Dates of stay:

Visiting from:

This is what I will remember most about my stay here:

Here is what I will recommend to other guests (restaurants, shopping, entertainment, etc.):

Message to Host:

Guest name:

Dates of stay:

Visiting from:

This is what I will remember most about my stay here:

Here is what I will recommend to other guests (restaurants, shopping, entertainment, etc.):

Message to Host:

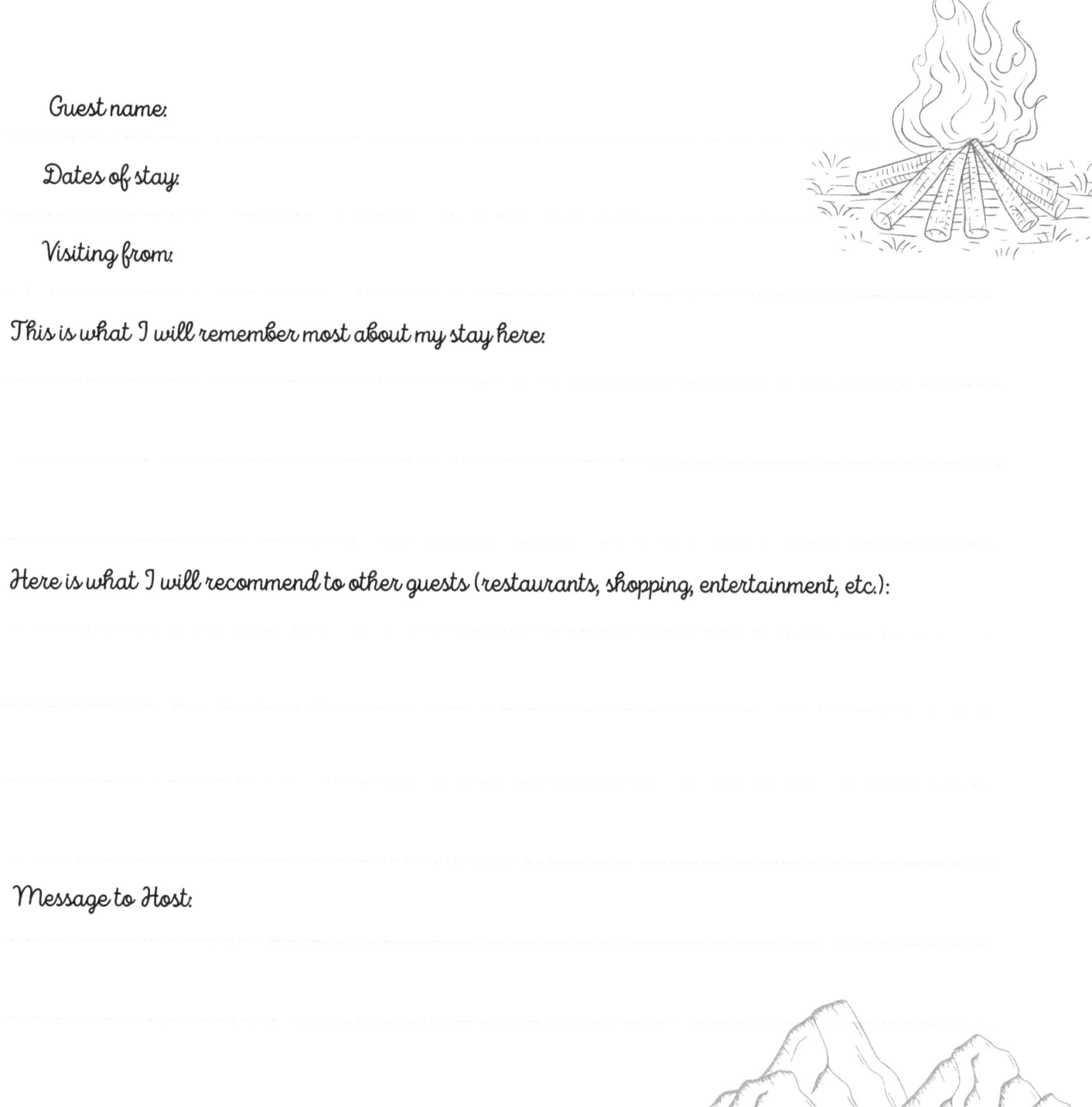

Guest name:

Dates of stay:

Visiting from:

This is what I will remember most about my stay here:

Here is what I will recommend to other guests (restaurants, shopping, entertainment, etc.):

Message to Host:

Guest name:

Dates of stay:

Visiting from:

This is what I will remember most about my stay here:

Here is what I will recommend to other guests (restaurants, shopping, entertainment, etc.):

Message to Host:

Guest name:

Dates of stay:

Visiting from:

This is what I will remember most about my stay here:

Here is what I will recommend to other guests (restaurants, shopping, entertainment, etc.):

Message to Host:

Guest name:

Dates of stay:

Visiting from:

This is what I will remember most about my stay here:

Here is what I will recommend to other guests (restaurants, shopping, entertainment, etc.):

Message to Host:

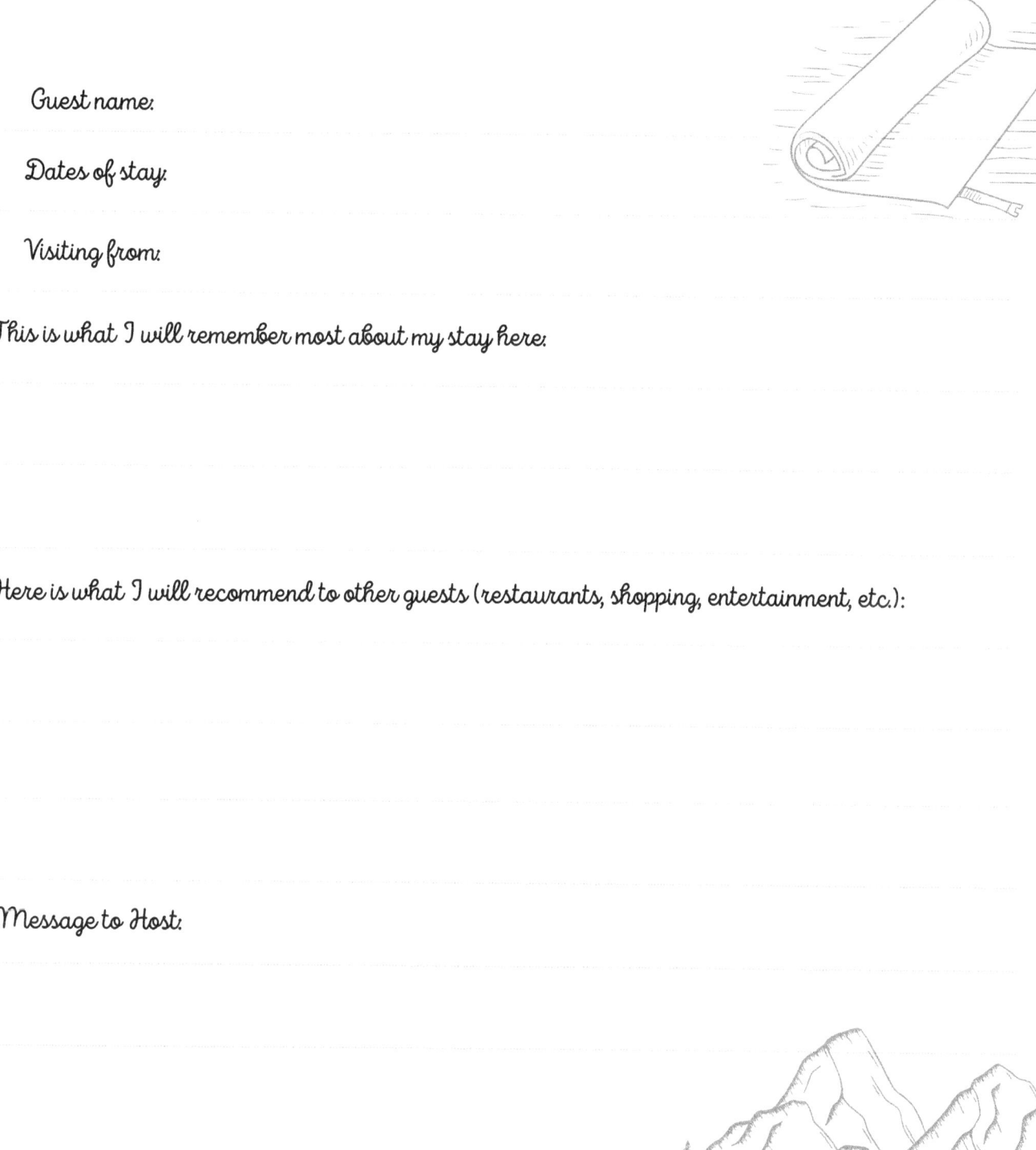

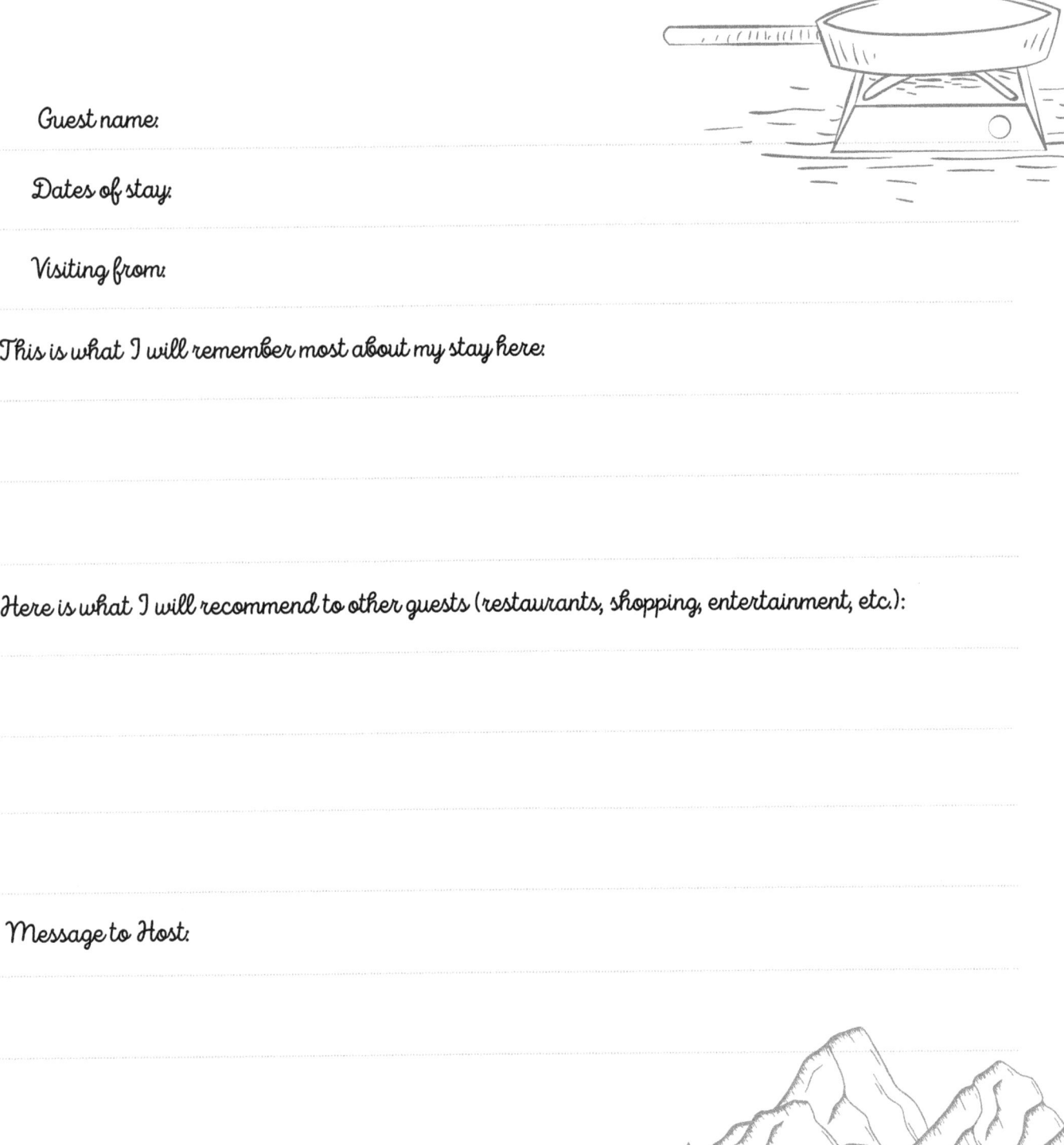

Guest name:

Dates of stay:

Visiting from:

This is what I will remember most about my stay here:

Here is what I will recommend to other guests (restaurants, shopping, entertainment, etc.):

Message to Host:

Guest name:

Dates of stay:

Visiting from:

This is what I will remember most about my stay here:

Here is what I will recommend to other guests (restaurants, shopping, entertainment, etc.):

Message to Host:

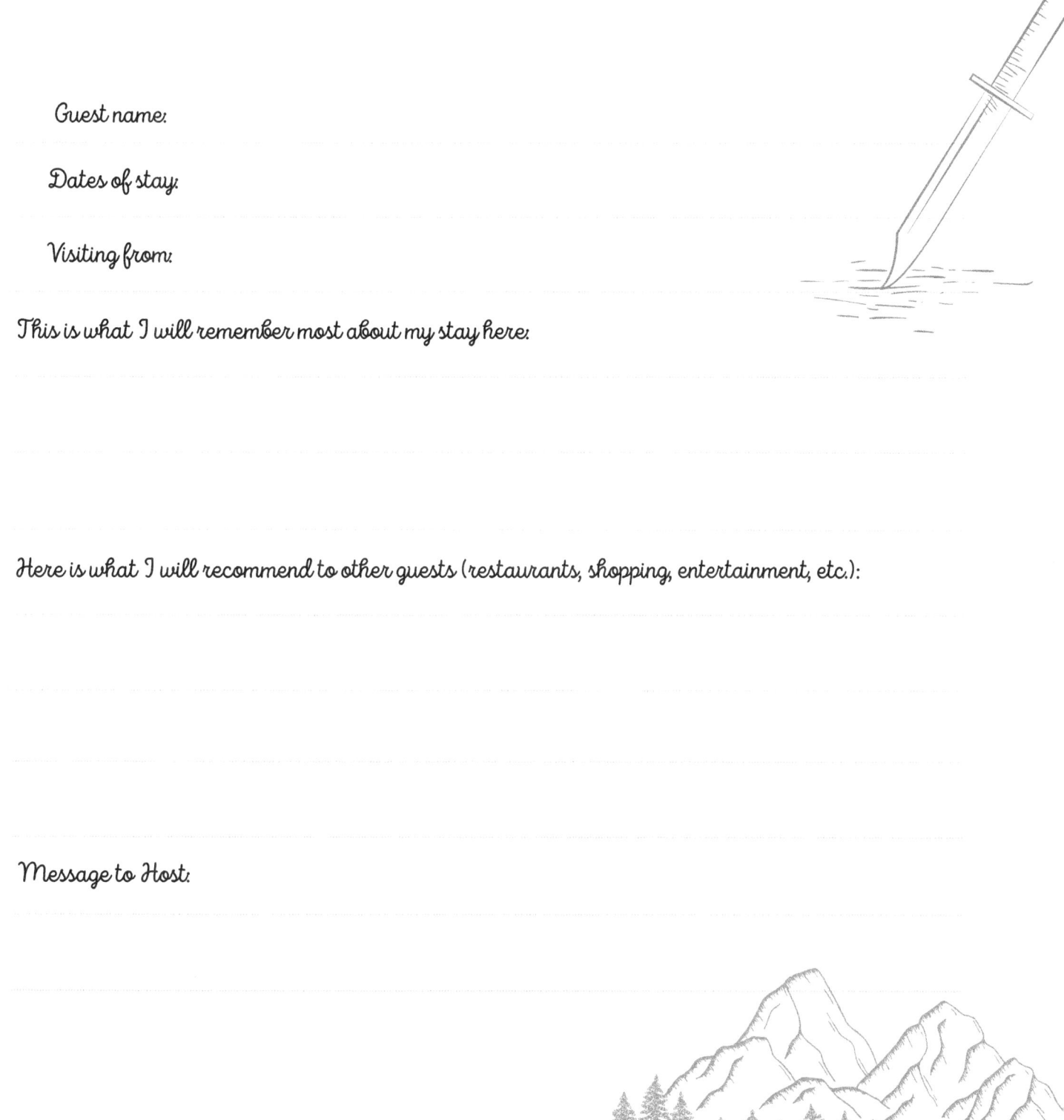

Guest name:

Dates of stay:

Visiting from:

This is what I will remember most about my stay here:

Here is what I will recommend to other guests (restaurants, shopping, entertainment, etc.):

Message to Host:

Guest name:

Dates of stay:

Visiting from:

This is what I will remember most about my stay here:

Here is what I will recommend to other guests (restaurants, shopping, entertainment, etc.):

Message to Host:

Guest name:

Dates of stay:

Visiting from:

This is what I will remember most about my stay here:

Here is what I will recommend to other guests (restaurants, shopping, entertainment, etc.):

Message to Host:

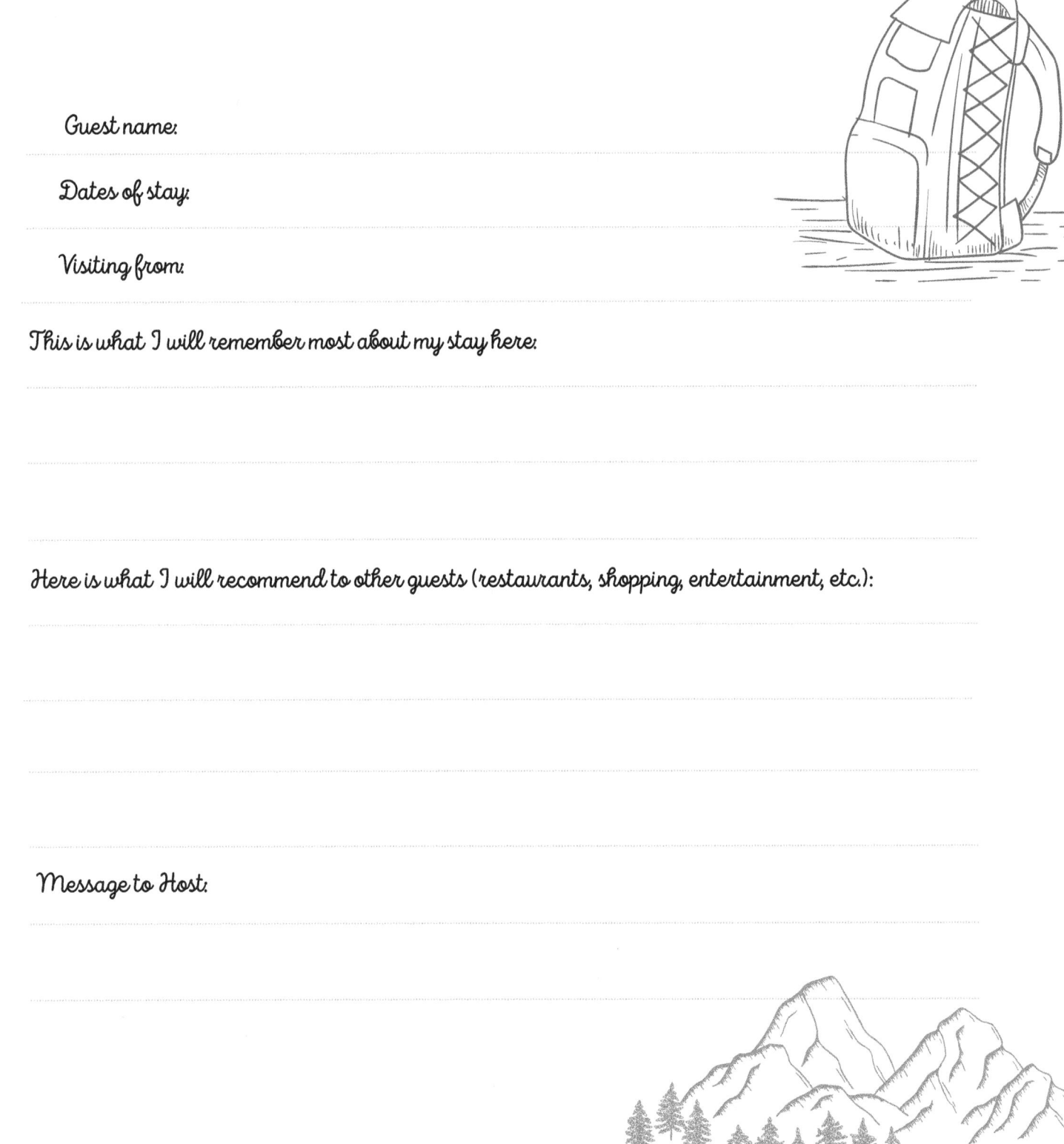

Guest name:

Dates of stay:

Visiting from:

This is what I will remember most about my stay here:

Here is what I will recommend to other guests (restaurants, shopping, entertainment, etc.):

Message to Host:

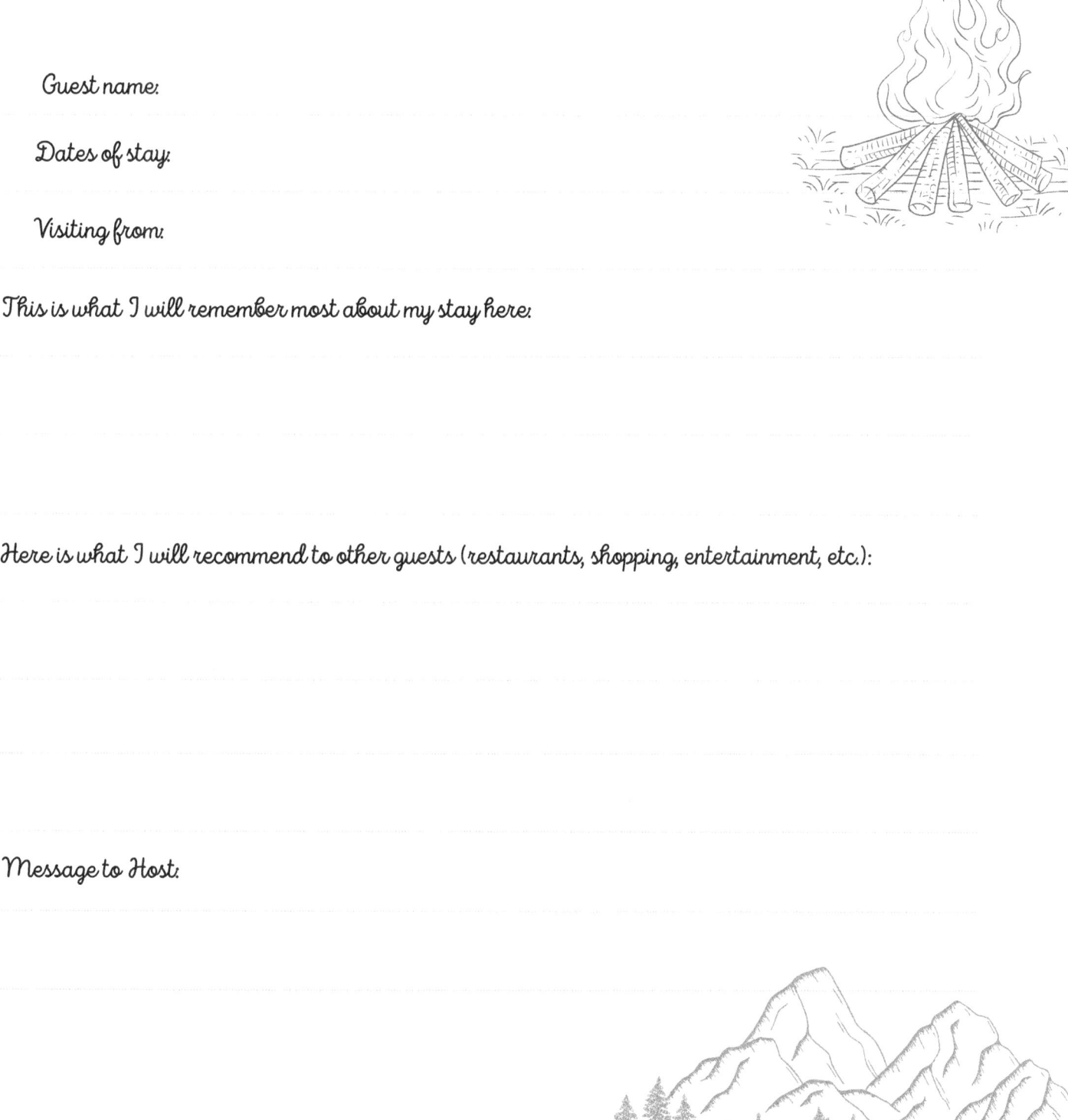

Guest name:

Dates of stay:

Visiting from:

This is what I will remember most about my stay here:

Here is what I will recommend to other guests (restaurants, shopping, entertainment, etc.):

Message to Host:

Guest name:

Dates of stay:

Visiting from:

This is what I will remember most about my stay here:

Here is what I will recommend to other guests (restaurants, shopping, entertainment, etc.):

Message to Host:

Guest name:

Dates of stay:

Visiting from:

This is what I will remember most about my stay here:

Here is what I will recommend to other guests (restaurants, shopping, entertainment, etc.):

Message to Host:

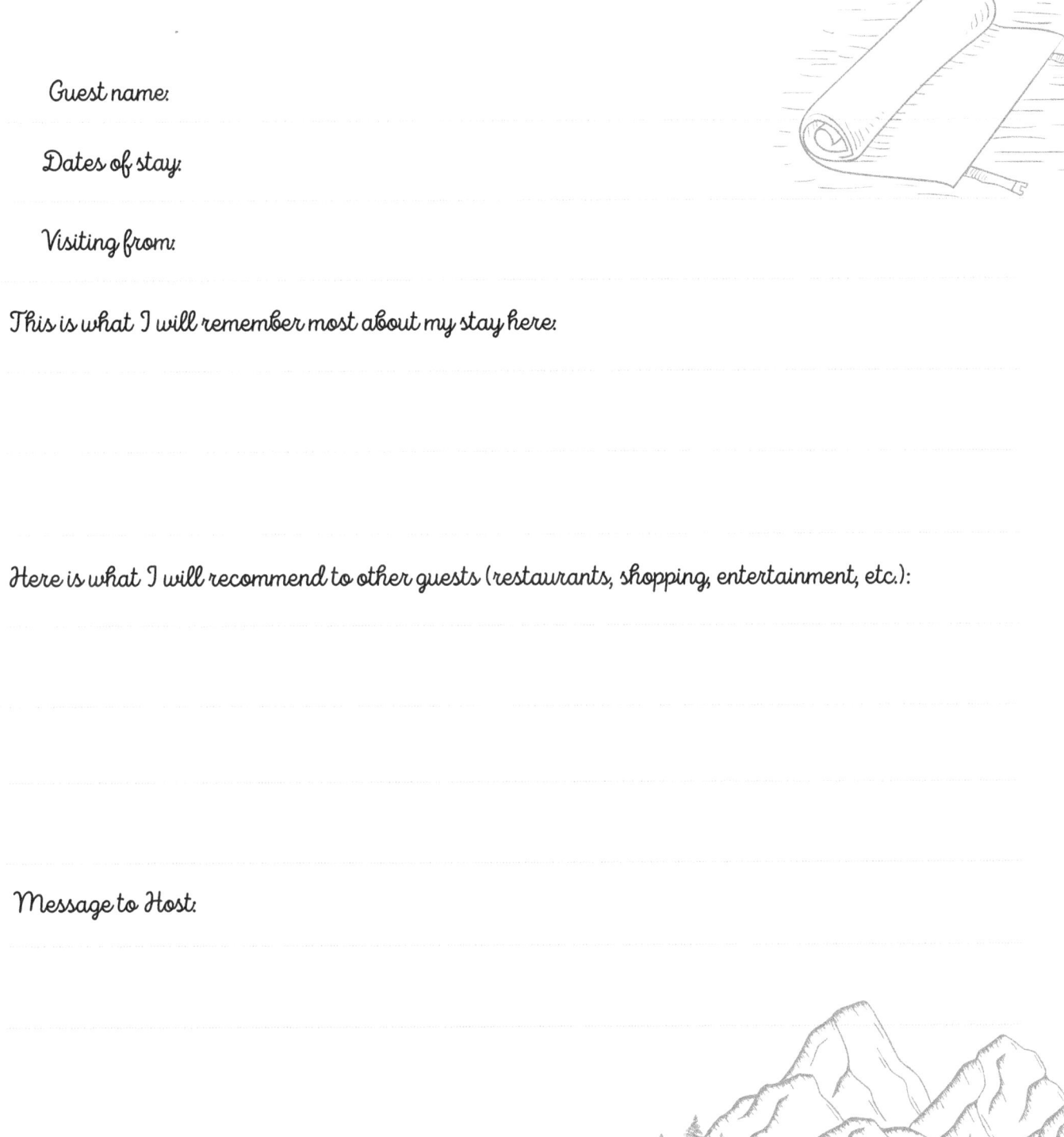

Guest name:

Dates of stay:

Visiting from:

This is what I will remember most about my stay here:

Here is what I will recommend to other guests (restaurants, shopping, entertainment, etc.):

Message to Host:

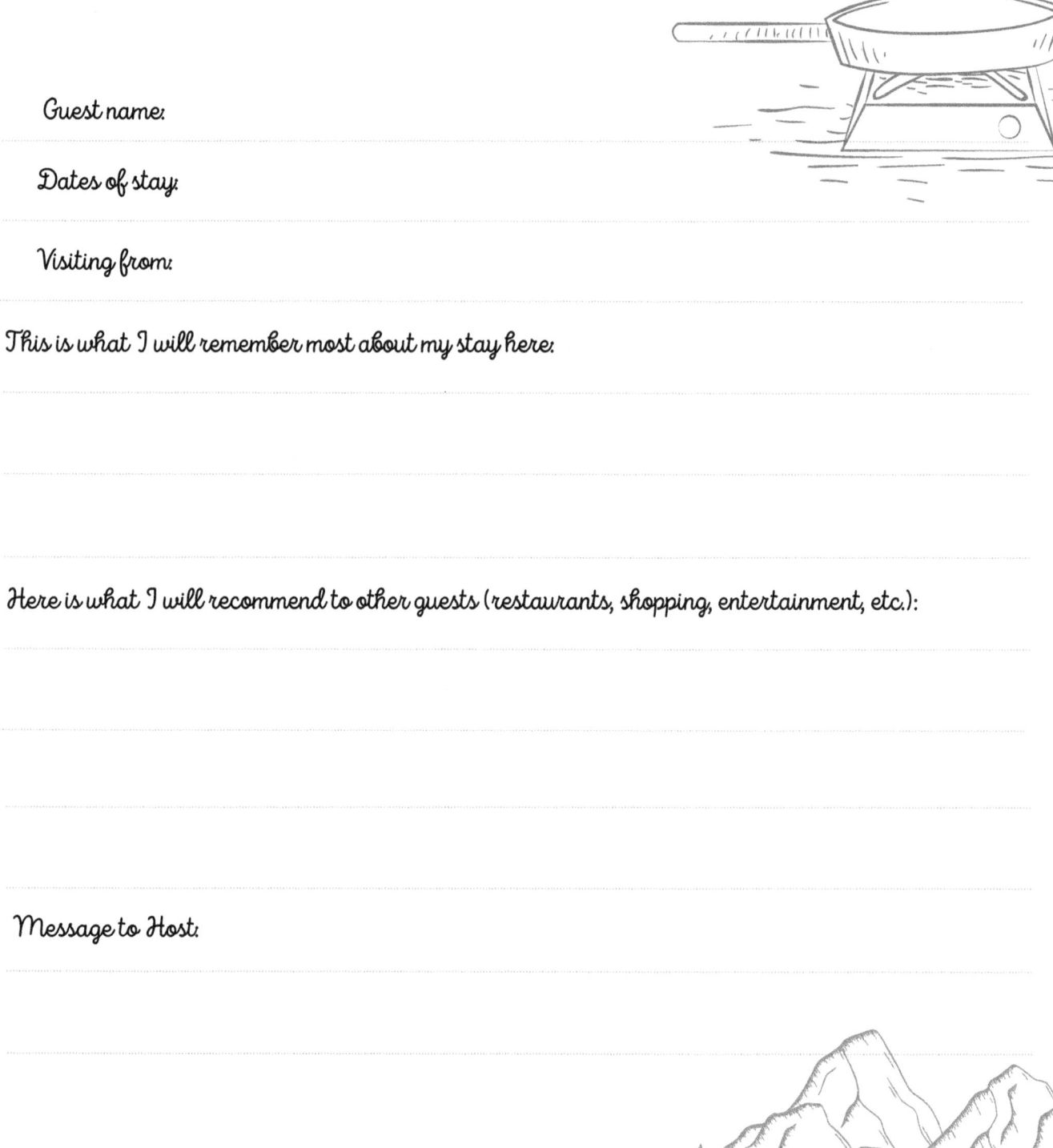

Guest name:

Dates of stay:

Visiting from:

This is what I will remember most about my stay here:

Here is what I will recommend to other guests (restaurants, shopping, entertainment, etc.):

Message to Host:

Guest name:

Dates of stay:

Visiting from:

This is what I will remember most about my stay here:

Here is what I will recommend to other guests (restaurants, shopping, entertainment, etc.):

Message to Host:

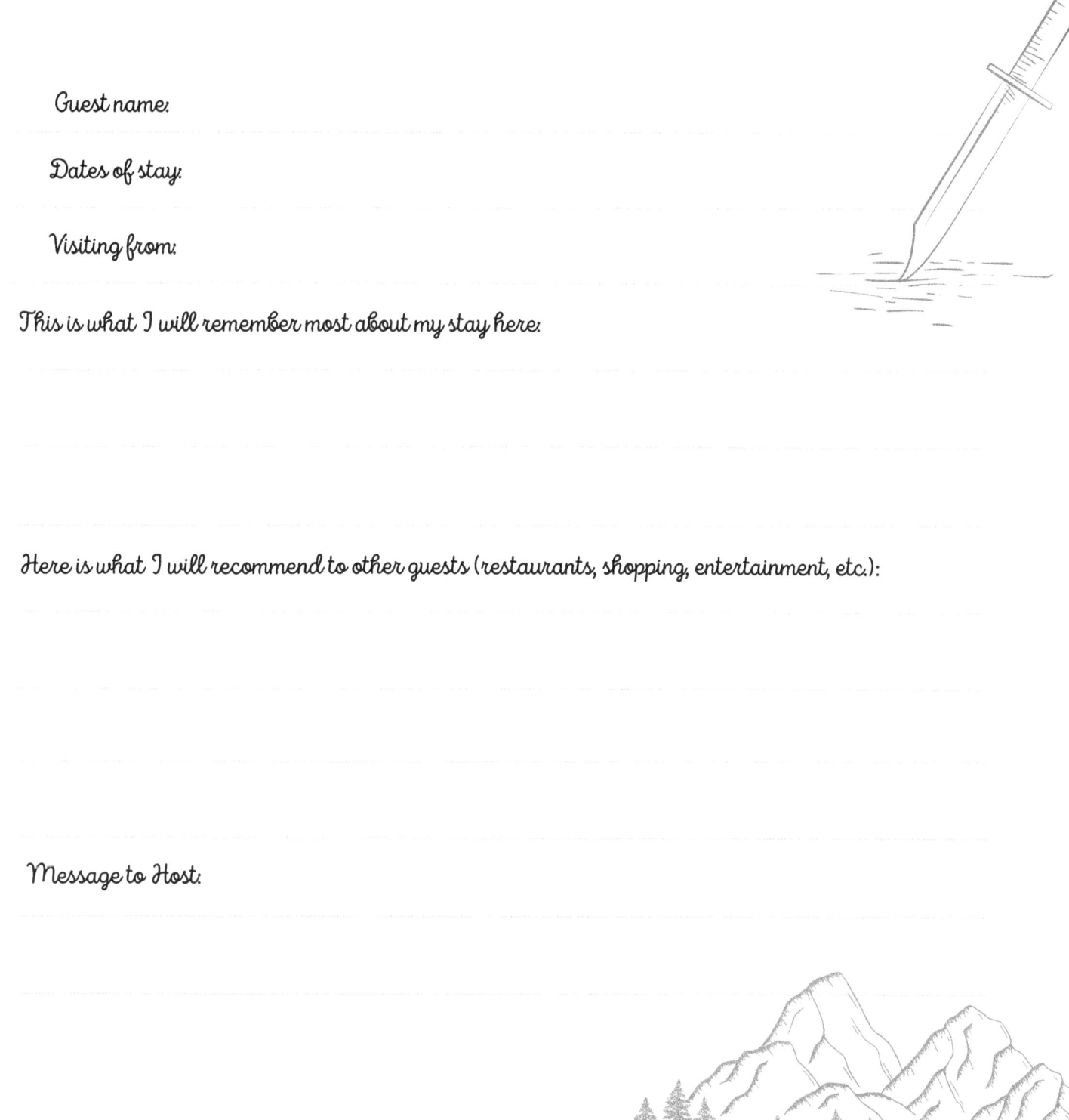

Guest name:

Dates of stay:

Visiting from:

This is what I will remember most about my stay here:

Here is what I will recommend to other guests (restaurants, shopping, entertainment, etc.):

Message to Host:

Copyrights 2021 - All rights reserved

You may not reproduce, duplicate, or send the contents of this book without direct written permission from the author. You cannot hereby despite any circumstance blame the publisher or hold him or her the legal responsibility for any reparation, compensation or monetary forfeiture owing to the information included herein, either in a direct or indirect way.

Legal Notice: This book has copyright protection. You can use the book for personal purpose. You should not sell, use, alter, distribute, quote, take excerpts or paraphrase in part of whole the material contained in this book without obtaining the permission of the author first.

Disclaimer Notice: You must take note that the information in this document is for casual reading and entertainment purpose only. We have made every attempt to provide accurate, up to date and reliable information. We do not express or imply guarantees of any kind. The person who read admit that the writer is not occupied in giving legal, financial, medical, or other advice. We put this book content by sourcing various places.

Please consult a licensed professional before you try any techniques shown in this book. By going through this document, the book lover comes to an agreement that under no situation is the author accountable for any forfeiture, direct or indirect, which they may incur because of the use of material contained in this document, including, but not limited to, - errors, omissions, or inaccuracies.

Thank you!

As a small family company, your feedback is very important to us.

Please let us know how you like our book at:

f /createpublication

◉ /createpublication

✉ createpublication@gmail.com

www.ingramcontent.com/pod-product-compliance
Lightning Source LLC
Chambersburg PA
CBHW080500240426
43673CB00006B/245